THE THRILL OF HOPE

THE THRILL OF HOPE

A COMMENTARY ON REVELATION

Bruce Green

ISBN-10: 1941972179
ISBN-13: 978-1941972175

Library of Congress Control Number: 2014950103

Published by Start2Finish Books
PO Box 680, Bowie, Texas 76230
www.start2finish.org

Printed in the United States of America

Cover Design: Josh Feit, Evangela.com

To Buck Dukes, Claude Flynn, and Cecil Langston:
three brothers who are an inspiration to me and countless others
through their patient endurance.

Special thanks to David Bogard, Cindy Hanson, Chris Tidwell, Alison James, and Janice Green for being generous with their time, encouraging in their words, and discerning in their thoughts through the helpful comments they provided on this book. It's better in many ways because of their contributions. Needless to say, whatever shortcomings exist are a reflection upon me rather than them.

CONTENTS

Part 5: The Beginning of the End (12-14) 129

Part 6: Judgment Day for Rome (15-20) 171

FOREWORD

"What am I going to do with Revelation?"

Who hasn't asked this question as they grew in their knowledge and understanding of other parts of God's word—only to flounder when it came to the book of Revelation? Feelings of satisfaction and accomplishment were muted by the book's intimidating presence.

If you have started Revelation a time or two but were unable to gain the traction needed to see it through to the end, *The Thrill of Hope* can help. It is an entry-level look at Revelation that puts the book in terms you can understand. There are devotional pieces that explain and develop its major themes, as well as FAQ sections that deal with specific issues of each chapter. You'll also find an emphasis on what Revelation says to disciples today.

Above all, it's my prayer that this book will help you to see the living hope that belongs to followers of the Lamb. It's my impression that Revelation often isn't pursued because it's perceived as not being worth the effort. Unlike James' letter, it is viewed as being of little practical value. Unlike the gospels, it's not looked upon as spiritual. I can't help thinking that, in the end, these objections say more about us than they do about Revelation. After all, while it may not be James or one of the gospels, God did see fit to give us the book! If we'll patiently work through Revelation (and let it work through us), we will be blessed as its original readers were (1:3).

May God richly bless you as you seek a greater knowledge of Him and His word. If you have thoughts, comments, or questions, send them to me at brucewgreen@gmail.com. I'd love to hear from you!

INTRODUCTION

Probably the biggest challenge most people have in approaching Revelation has to do with getting some sort of handle on it. It's so different from anything else they've ever seen or heard that it's natural for them to feel overwhelmed by it. Is there a way of looking at Revelation that makes it more user-friendly?

I think there is. If you're familiar with the classic movie, *The Wizard of Oz,* I believe you can grasp the basic framework of Revelation.[1] By suggesting this parallel, I have no wish to trivialize the book or suggest it's no more than something along the lines of a fantasy movie. What I am saying is that the movie and book intersect at certain points, and that convergence can be useful in getting a grip on Revelation.

To begin with, both have similar structure and content. The movie starts off with Dorothy on a farm in Kansas. For the time in which it was made (1939), life on the farm was something just about everyone could relate to. If you didn't live on the farm, your parents or grandparents did.

---

1. This idea came to me from Dorothy Rossing's book, *The Rapture Exposed.* Ms. Rossing offers Dickens' *A Christmas Carol,* as a way for us to think about the book of Revelation. She points out that just as Scrooge's dream about Marley, and the ghosts of Christmas Past, Present & Future jolted him into changing his life, so Revelation should be thought of as a book of visions that seeks to inspire faithfulness in the lives of its recipients. What I really gravitated toward though were the more casual references she made to *The Wizard of Oz.* To me, it provides an even better framework for relating to Revelation.

In the same way, Revelation begins in a normal manner (for first-century churches) with John addressing seven churches in Asia (chapters 1-3). Although we'll see that the content of these messages is specialized due to the unique circumstances the congregations were facing, their form is nonetheless very much like a compressed version of what we find in the letters of the New Testament.

If the movie and book begin in a normal manner, what follows is anything but ordinary. In the *The Wizard of Oz* the tornado strikes, and Dorothy has this spectacular dream involving flying houses and monkeys, witches that are good, wicked, and dead, munchkins, a yellow brick road, an Emerald City, a lion that walks on two feet and talks, as do a scarecrow and a tin man. It's all mind-boggling, and yet most of us aren't even fazed by it because we're familiar with the movie, and we understand it's all a part of Dorothy's dream.

Revelation's development is along the same lines. With the fourth chapter, the vision aspect of the book shifts from present to future, and we see all sorts of things: creatures with eyes all over, a lamb with seven horns and seven eyes, locusts that resemble humans and horses, a dragon, a beast coming out of the sea, and a beast coming out of the earth. And that's just a fraction of what is revealed. If you read through the book in one sitting, you could easily suffer from image overload. And yet, if you think about it, John's not doing anything different than what we encounter in *The Wizard of Oz.*

Both expose the oppressor. In *The Rapture Exposed,* Dorothy Rossing parallels Dorothy's dog, Toto, pulling the curtain open to reveal an ordinary man (rather than "the Great Oz") with John showing through Revelation that neither Rome nor Domitian is to be feared or worshipped because neither ultimately has any real power. I think that's exactly the case! We could also add the Wicked Witch of the West's meltdown runs right along the same tracks as the beast, prophet, and devil being cast into the lake of fire. Revelation clearly shows that while the oppressor (and others) may think and act as though they are omnipotent, they are not.

Instead, victory belongs to Jesus and those who steadfastly follow Him.

Both use their dream or vision as a vehicle for communicating their overarching message. Everything in Dorothy's dream helps her to see the truth, "There's no place like home." As the movie begins, she's suffering from teenage angst. She would rather be anywhere than where she is (stuck on a farm in Kansas). She wistfully sings "Somewhere Over the Rainbow." But after she has experienced all of the terror and magic of Oz, she concludes that somewhere over the rainbow is not there but back on the farm in Kansas. She clicks her ruby slippers together, says the magic words, and she's home.

In the same way, Revelation was written to show Christians there's no power like hope. As John will demonstrate, Satan is the ultimate evil and force behind Rome. The oppressive circumstances faced by the disciples have already cost one follower of Jesus his life and will result in the death of others (Revelation 2:13; 6:9-11). What can produce the patient endurance John repeatedly calls for (1:9; 3:10; 13:10; 14:12)? It is the hope they have through Jesus—from the risen Christ's assurance that He holds the keys of death and Hades, to His promise of making all things new.

If you haven't had a handle on Revelation, I hope this gives you a place to start and the confidence that you can understand this book!

FAQ

Revelation is so controversial and seems capable of being understood so many different ways. What chance does an ordinary person have of making sense of it?

If this is the way you think or feel, I can understand why. At the same time, you should know that you are exactly the person for whom this book was written. Let me share with you a couple of things that are said in the first three verses of Revelation that make it clear we can understand this book.

John begins by speaking of "The revelation from Jesus Christ," (v. 1). The word "revelation" is a translation of the Greek word "apocalypse," which literally means "unveiling." It has to do with making something known that was previously a mystery. Think of a statue or painting that is covered with a canvas until its public exhibition. While it's covered, you can't tell very much about it. You can only get a general sense of its size and shape. But when the canvas comes off, you can see it for what it is. This is the import of the word the Spirit guided John to use in speaking of his message, and it suggests the very opposite of the idea that the book cannot be understood. Somewhere along the line, we either have to start believing this or quit calling it "Revelation."

The other point is not as commonly made, but I think speaks just as clearly. It is that John is writing to seven churches in Asia (v. 4), and he pronounces a blessing on the one who reads Revelation and those who hear it "and take to heart what is written in it," (v. 3 NIV). None of this is possible if the book is incomprehensible. God isn't playing games with us; the book's blessing is just as attainable today as it was in the first century.

Is this book about the future? Are there parts that haven't been fulfilled?

Although it's tempting, we should avoid thinking of Revelation exclusively (or even primarily) as a book of predictions. Approaching it in such a manner is like thinking about a wonderful meal only in terms of the dishes it is served on. While the predictive element certainly exists and is important, it's not the central aspect of the message and shouldn't be our major takeaway from the book.

As to the time of those predictions, John tells his first-century audience at the beginning and end of Revelation that the things he is writing about will happen soon (1:1, 3; 22:6; 22:10). Take a moment to read these verses and then ask yourself, "Does it sound like he is telling his readers that the fulfillment of what he's writing about will happen thousands of years in the future, or is it something they should expect to see in their lifetime?" The answer isn't hard, is it? (I won't pretend that everything in Revelation is this simple).

Bracketing the beginning and end in this way is known as an *inclusio*, a literary device common to Scripture that draws the reader's attention to something important (see Matthew 1:23; 28:20; Romans 1:5; 16:26 for a couple of examples of this). One of the places to begin understanding Revelation is by accepting what John has to say about the time or context and the emphasis he gives to it.

But how can this book be fulfilled if Jesus hasn't returned since there are several references to His coming?

Good question! (I told you everything in Revelation isn't simple).

Actually though, the answer here isn't terribly difficult; we just have to tweak our thinking a little bit in regard to how we understand the word "coming." When we hear this word, we think of the return of Jesus at the end of time (Acts 1:9-11; Hebrews 9:27-28). But the word is also used many times in Scripture when the final return of Jesus isn't in view. Take a look at John 14:18, 23 and see if the "coming" there doesn't sound more like God and Jesus dwelling in the believer through the Holy Spirit rather than the appearing of Christ at the end of time. Then notice that Jesus tells the church at Ephesus that if they don't repent, He will come to them and remove their lamp stand (Revelation 2:5). Since the final return of the Lord obviously isn't dependent upon whether some disciples in first-century Ephesus changed some things about their lives, it's clear that "coming" in this text doesn't refer to the ultimate one. There's more of this kind of thing in 2:16 and 3:3, 11.

What does all of this mean? We'll develop that more as we go through Revelation, but for right now, just note that "coming" doesn't always refer to the final return of Jesus.

PART ONE

Jesus to His Church

This section functions as an introduction (Revelation 1), then quickly moves to individualized messages for seven churches in the province of Asia (Revelation 2-3). The book begins with a brief explanation from John concerning his writing, followed by a greeting to the churches. After this, we see Jesus commissioning John to, "Write what you see in a book and send it to the seven churches," (1:11). John then records Christ's message to each of the seven churches. His words give us a clear picture of the challenges facing these congregations as well as how they were responding to them.

The revelation to John (1:1-3)
John to the seven churches (1:4-8)
Jesus appears to John (1:9-20)
Jesus speaks to the seven churches (2:1-3:22)

HOPE

"When I saw him, I fell at his feet as though dead. But he laid his right hand on me, saying, 'Fear not, I am the first and the last, and the living one. I died, and behold I am alive forevermore, and I have the keys of Death and Hades'" **(1:17-18).**

Disciple or not, everyone has heard of Revelation (even if they refer to it as "Revelations") and has a take on it (even though it might be bewilderment).

But if novelty is associated with the book, it is not what defines or drives it. Despite the distortions placed upon it by television evangelists, the *Left Behind* industry, and numerous others, John's letter offers great spiritual enrichment if we are willing to learn the language he speaks and step into the world he describes. As you can tell from the title of this book, I think it has much to offer us in the way of hope. Although the word is not mentioned once in the book's 22 chapters, you can feel its pull on every page.

In the first chapter of Revelation, John has an incredible vision of Jesus that scares him to death. Christ places His hand on him to reassure John (and us) that we don't need to be afraid of anything, even death. Our Lord was dead, but now is alive "for ever and ever" (1:18 NIV). And He has authority over death and the grave. In a word, we have hope.

Why is this so important? Because we live in a world that is long on hype and short on hope. The counterfeit kind is passed around everywhere in currency ranging from more stuff to more status. But just as all legitimate money is traceable to the Federal Treasury, all true hope comes from God. You don't win it in a lottery; it comes only through Jesus (1 Peter 1:3).

There's a grave marker in a cemetery in Albuquerque, NM, over the spot where five-year-old Billy Ducott was laid to rest after his brief life was ended by Burkitt's lymphoma. In the course of fighting the disease, Billy was taken to Children's Hospital in Boston for treatment that ultimately proved unsuccessful. The family's wish was for Billy to be taken home to die, but his condition had deteriorated to such an extent that this seemed impossible until Dr. Hope Druckman, a pediatric resident, offered to accompany Billy and his parents on the flight back to Albuquerque.

Their plan hit a snag when they made connections in Dallas, and the airline refused to allow Billy to board due to his worsening condition. They spent the night at a local hospital, where Dr. Druckman tried for two hours to get Billy on an Air Force medevac flight. Finally, someone remembered there was a local surgeon who owned a small plane, and she called him at 1:00 am. After hearing Billy's story, he agreed to help, although his plane was too small to take everyone.

Early the next morning, Dr. Druckman and Billy departed in the private plane, while his parents took a commercial flight. When they all landed in Albuquerque, Billy was taken to a local hospital where, surrounded by his family, he peacefully passed from this life. The marker over his grave bears his name, the date of his birth and death, and these words: "Hope brought him home."[1]

What was true for Billy Ducott is true for us. In life, death, or anything in between, hope will bring us home. That's the story John would have us see in Revelation.

---

1. Billy's story, written by Ted Kohler, appeared in *Readers' Digest* in January of 1985, under the title, "Hope Brought Him Home."

QUESTIONS

1. Dostoevsky said, "To live without hope is to cease to live." How is this true?
2. How is our world "long on hype and short on hope?"
3. What makes our hope in Jesus different from other hopes?

BLESSING

"Blessed is the one who reads aloud the words of this prophecy, and blessed are those who hear, and who keep what is written in it, for the time is near" **(1:3).**

Someone can tell you about a book or a movie, and you can appreciate it at a certain level. But if you are really interested, you won't be satisfied to live off the experience of others; you'll have to read/see it for yourself, won't you? I think that's the way it is with God's word—even the harder-to-understand parts, like the book of Revelation.

We're greatly blessed to be able to consult the work of scholars and be enriched by their efforts and insights. But for all of that, there should be a desire to make the book our own. This means we wrestle with the text until, in the words of Alexander Campbell, we can come within "understanding distance" of it. That doesn't mean we exhaustively understand it or can even necessarily explain it to others. What it does mean is that we invest the sweat equity in it so that we have a basic understanding of the book and its overall message. It seems that this is part of what John means when he pronounces a blessing on those who "hear it and take to heart what is written, " (1:3; 22:7 NIV).

At some point, you will probably be tempted to read the devotional pieces and bypass the text, but you must be strong and resist! I understand how an initial reading of any part of Revelation may seem fruitless, possibly even resulting in more confusion than clarity. Keep in mind that the learning curve is always steepest at the start. Hang in there with the book, and I promise you will slowly but surely learn its language.

It will take some time though. Revelation is not given to a quick glance here and there. It must be slowly cooked rather than microwaved. But if you are patient, you will be rewarded with a great feast.

Don't let anyone (including yourself) rob you of the blessing God has for you in Revelation!

QUESTIONS

1. Give some examples of things that you want to experience personally (as opposed to merely hearing about them from others).
2. What does it mean to come within "understanding distance" of Scripture?
3. What kind of commitment are you willing to make toward understanding Revelation?

NEVER HAS BEEN AND NEVER WILL BE

"To him who loves us and has freed us from our sins by his blood" (1:5).

It's one of those old Hallmark commercials—the kind that are two minutes plus and shown only during Hallmark Hall of Fame presentations. I've long since forgotten what the presentation was, but I haven't forgotten the commercial. It's called "Home for the Holidays."[1]

It's a snowy Christmas Eve, and there is an extended family gathering at the grandparents' home. Ten-year-old Johnny and his parents are there, as well as a Christmas card from his older brother Tom, who is working in Europe. The card says he will be home for Christmas Eve in time for him and Johnny to sing for the family as they do each year.

The weather worsens as the day goes on, and other relatives are barely able to get in through the storm. As afternoon turns into evening, everyone has managed to make it, except Tom. No one has heard anything from him. It is a disappointed Johnny who dutifully stands before the family and begins to sing "O Holy Night."

He's not too far into the song when a door opens behind him and Tom steps in. He holds up a finger so everyone will keep quiet and walks

1. If you're interested in watching this, it was available on YouTube at the time of this writing.

up behind Johnny. The solo becomes a duet as he puts his arm on his shoulder, and they sing:

A thrill of hope—the weary world rejoices,
For yonder breaks a new and glorious morn.
Fall on your knees! O Hear the angels' voices!
O night divine! O night when Christ was born.

There was a time for mankind when the world was frozen in a winter of sin and despair. Misery was the order of the season and hope was in full retreat. Just when things were at their bleakest, and defeat seemed inevitable, our older brother arrived on the scene. He put His arm on our shoulder, joy in our song, and the world has never been the same.

Deity came to earth in the person of Jesus. The little baby lying in the feeding trough, the one among the animals, is Lord of heaven and earth. And He grew to be a man who, in John's words, "loves us and has freed us from our sins by his blood" (1:5). "Couldn't be," you say. "The Sovereign of the universe would never subject Himself to such things as mangers and crosses."

But He did. And we're the reason.

This is the star that should guide us and fill our lives with meaning and purpose. This far-fetched, amazing life that began in a stable, ended on a cross, and then began again in a garden is our story, our hope, and our redemption.

What began in Bethlehem couldn't be contained in that tiny town. It spilled over into Galilee, Samaria, and Jerusalem. Then it was on to Athens, Alexandria, and Rome. The centuries have been unable to hold the glorious truth of that life, and it lives today, brightly beaming its healing light to a hurting world. You see, there is simply not enough darkness in the universe to extinguish the light of His life.

Never has been and never will be.

QUESTIONS

1. What do you think is the significance of John mentioning Jesus' love for us and His freeing us from our sins being mentioned together in 1:5? What does this tell us about our redemption?
2. In what ways is sin the opposite of love?
3. How is it true that "there is not enough darkness in the universe to extinguish the light of His life?"

FAITHFUL WITNESSES

"I, John, your brother and partner in the tribulation and the kingdom and the patient endurance that are in Jesus, was on the island called Patmos on account of the word of God and the testimony of Jesus" **(1:9).**

The words "witness," "testimony," and "testify" are used a total of sixteen times in Revelation. However, their significance is even greater than that number would suggest, and in the first chapter, this theme is introduced as we're told that John is on Patmos "on account of the word of God and the testimony of Jesus." This could mean that he is there to receive the vision (Richard Bauckham, *The Theology of the Book of Revelation*). However, I think the usage of these terms throughout the rest of the book (see especially 6:9; 20:4) would indicate that he is there because he has been a faithful witness. As a result, John has been banished to the island or possibly fled there. To this end, he speaks of himself as "your brother and companion in the suffering and the kingdom" (v. 9 NIV). Notice that whatever else the kingdom might be, it is not incompatible with suffering.

We're also told that John "testifies to everything he saw—that is, the word of God and the testimony of Jesus Christ" (v. 2 NIV). This phrase, "the testimony of Jesus," resonates throughout Revelation. It speaks of the core truths concerning Jesus (the kind of things John shares in v. 5-7). In

12:17, John tells us that the dragon goes off to wage war against "those who keep the commandments of God and hold to the testimony of Jesus." In 19:10, the angel tells John not to worship him, for "I am a fellow servant with you and your brothers who hold to the testimony of Jesus." Another passage says, "I saw the souls of those who had been beheaded for the testimony of Jesus and for the word of God" (20:4).

It's hard to read these texts (and others like it) without getting the impression that the "the testimony of Jesus" is a central theme of Revelation. Disciples bear witness to the truths of Jesus through their actions and words, something John will return to throughout the book. As Jesus addresses the seven churches (Revelation 2-3), much of what He has to say to them centers on whether they are reflecting these truths (like Antipas, "my faithful witness," 2:13), or compromising them (like the church at Thyatira, 2:20ff). In the more visionary section of the book (Revelation 4-22) we've already seen Satan (the dragon) attacking those who hold the testimony of Jesus (12:17), and we learn the crucial truth that people overcome him "by the word of their testimony" (12:11).

In all of this, disciples are being called to align themselves with their Lord, who is recognized as being "the faithful witness" (1:5). As a human, He was and is the centerpiece of what it means to live a God-centered existence of love and submission. As such, He is "the faithful and true witness" (3:14). Disciples in Revelation are called to follow in His steps, even if, as in the case of Jesus, it leads to death (2:10).

Revelation isn't a gentle call for nice Christian people to be nicer Christian people (it's not a sermonette speaking to Christianettes). It's not even about challenging first-century followers of Jesus to get out of their comfort zones—they were already living far outside those! Revelation is a bugle call breaking through the haze and chaos of battle urging them not to retreat from the front lines, but to keep their banners raised high for Jesus.

Understanding and applying Revelation today is much more than sifting through its images and understanding what God is saying through these things. It is strapping on the armor of Christ and living courageously in a culture that is increasingly dark and hostile. It is living as faithful witnesses.

Just like our Lord.

QUESTIONS

1. What is "the testimony of Jesus?" How is it fundamental to Revelation?
2. How does "the testimony of Jesus" relate to our lives today?
3. How is Jesus the ultimate faithful witness?

THAT'S OUR LORD!

"Then I turned to see the voice that was speaking to me, and on turning I saw seven golden lampstands, and in the midst of the lampstands one like a son of man" **(1:12-13).**

Whatever else it might be, Revelation is a book of pictures! Truths are more often communicated through the images John receives rather than spelled out for him in regular speech. If we don't come to grips with this, we won't be able to understand the book.

The first chapter is a good example of this. Grace and peace are extended to the seven churches by the Godhead (vv. 4-5). God and the Spirit are identified in a manner that is consistent with the overall style of the book. But the focus is obviously on Jesus. In vv. 5-6, we're told that He is:

- the faithful witness,
- the firstborn of the dead,
- the ruler of kings on earth,
- the One who loves us and has freed us from our sins by His blood,
- the One who made us a kingdom,
- the One who made us priests.

That's what we're given in straightforward (albeit theologically-loaded) terms. Then in vv. 12-20, John relates to us a vision he has of the risen Christ. It complements and illustrates the truths we've been told, as well as provides imagery for Jesus' messages to the churches in Revelation 2-3. While an item-by-item analysis of the different elements of the vision has its place, one of the most helpful truths concerns the primary source of the imagery.

This vision of Jesus combines two figures from a vision the prophet Daniel has in Daniel 7 (the Ancient of Days, 7:9ff; the Son of Man, 7:13). There the Ancient of Days passes judgment on an immoral and oppressive fourth kingdom and grants everlasting dominion to the Son of Man (vv. 13-14). Since Daniel is writing in the time of the first kingdom (Babylon) during the reign of Belshazzar (c. 553 B.C., 7:1), his dream is obviously predictive and stretches centuries into the future. By Christ being identified with these two figures, John's readers would see Him as the fulfillment of Daniel's vision and understand the fourth kingdom to be Rome. Jesus is the conqueror who has taken the Empire's best shot through the crucifixion, and rather than being vanquished, He has returned to stand among the churches (the lampstands). Rome will fare no better against His people than they did against Him. What a message! What a Lord!

Christ stands among churches (then and today) and sees us through. Make no mistake about it: what makes us special is not our spirituality, insight, abilities, etc. It's our Lord!

QUESTIONS

1. It's pointed out that in Revelation "truth is communicated through ... images." What exactly does this mean? Can you think of examples from Scripture where image-speech is used?
2. What is the significance of the picture of Jesus in John's vision coming from Daniel 7?
3. How is Christ standing among the churches good news for us?

THE ONE WHO HOLDS THE STARS

"In his right hand he held seven stars..." **(1:16).**

The opening picture of Jesus in Revelation is a breathtaking one. It's not the Jesus we're used to seeing in paintings and pictures. From the way He's described by John, it's clearly impressionistic (N. T. Wright, *Revelation for Everyone*), and meant to convey certain truths about Christ rather than portray His physical likeness. For example, His eyes are described as being "like blazing fire" (1:14 NIV). Since fire is often associated with judgment in the Scripture (Leviticus 10:1-2; 2 Kings 1:10, 12, 14), I think we're supposed to see the fire in His eyes as His wrath primarily toward those who are oppressing His people (Revelation 6:9-11). This is Rome under the emperor Domitian.

The other aspects of Jesus' description can be treated in the same way. We can look to the Scriptures, find examples of similar usage, and arrive at a sense of what is being conveyed. That is true for all elements of the picture except one—where Jesus is said to hold seven stars in His hand (1:16). As Richard Oster has pointed out in his *Seven Congregations in a Roman Crucible,* there's nothing that corresponds to this anywhere in the Scriptures.

What we do know is that Domitian had a son who lived only a few years. Sometime after his death, Domitian had a coin minted that showed his son seated atop the world with arms outstretched, hands open, and seven stars around him. The inscription on the coin reads, "The divine Caesar, son of the emperor Domitian." Here, then, by Roman reckoning is a divine son who rules the world.

It seems quite likely that John's description of Jesus as "the ruler of kings on earth" (v. 5), who holds seven stars in his hand (v. 16), is formed in response to the coin minted by Domitian.[1] It is to say: This is the true divine Son who rules the world. Rome could mint their coins and make their proclamations, but it didn't change the fact that the emperor's son was dead and in his grave, and Domitian was powerless to do anything about it. The coin might have been real, but its message was counterfeit. Meanwhile, the One who died on a Roman cross was alive forever and ever and holding the keys to death and Hades (1:18).

What a powerful message for the struggling churches of Asia. What a timely reminder for us today. The One who holds the stars holds our hope!

QUESTIONS

1. What does it mean to say that that picture John sees of Jesus is impressionistic?
2. What reason is there for thinking that the vision John sees of Jesus might be an answer to the way Domitian's son was displayed on a Roman coin?
3. What kind of an impact do you think this would have made upon the disciples John is writing to? What does it say to us?

---

1. If John is writing during the time of Vespasian (which I believe he is), then it is even more impressive as it is formed in response to something that has not yet happened. Vespasian rules from A.D. 69-79, Titus from 79-81, and Domitian from 81-96. Roll that around in your mind a bit!

FAQ

Shouldn't Revelation be interpreted literally? If we don't take it literally, are we honoring God and taking Him seriously?

Revelation should be interpreted like any other work of literature—in the manner its author intended! That being so, it's a huge mistake to conclude that there is one type of speech that is inherently more serious or God-honoring than another (see Hebrews 1:1). Would we think of telling a loved one they could only communicate to us in a certain manner of speech? Stated another way, it is just as dishonoring to God to literalize figurative speech as it is to figurize literal speech.

How did John intend for his readers to understand Revelation?

He tells us something important in v. 1 when he says, "He sent and **signified it** by his angel unto his servant John" (ASV, cf. KJV, NKJV, NASU marg.). The words in bold print are the translation of *esemanen* (from *semaino*). That's the verb form of the word John uses over and over in his gospel for the "signs" (*semeion*) that Jesus did. Those signs are more than miracles; they are miracles with a message. They signify something (John 20:30-31).

In John 6, He feeds the crowd with loaves and fishes, and tells them that He is the bread of life. In John 8, He proclaims He is the light of the world and then gives sight to a blind man (John 9). In John 11, He raises

Lazarus from the dead and speaks of Himself as the resurrection and the life. With all of these, we're not supposed to stop at the signs, but to look past them to the truth they proclaim. The sign (miracle) isn't the message; what it signifies is the message.

The NIV and ESV's translation of Revelation 1:1 miss out on this important truth John is sharing. Both of them read, "He made it known by sending his angel to his servant John." That's like saying someone who is signing for the hearing-impaired is making known the message. While that's certainly true, it's a wandering generality compared to the specific meaning of the word "signing." "Made it known" tells us they communicated, but "signed" tells us how they communicated. In the same way, John is telling us that God made the message known by signifying it through His angel to John. This is of critical importance because we're entering a book of pictures, symbols, and representations. To try to literalize them is to disregard what we've been told; it's to ignore the instructions we've been given.

Is the "coming" spoken of in 1:7 the final return of Jesus?

I don't think we're meant to understand it that way. Take a look at Daniel 7:13 and ask yourself if the "coming" spoken of there is the return of Jesus at the end of time, because this is where John takes this from (with the rest of the passage coming from Zechariah 12:10). Just as in the Daniel text, this is a coming in judgment upon Rome. We're told that "all peoples on earth will mourn because of Him" (NIV), but we're not to literalize that either. In Revelation, the people of the earth are associated with Rome (3:10; 6:10; 8:13; 11:10, etc.), while God's people are associated with heaven (12:12; 13:6). What we're being told here and in 22:12, 20 (making it another *inclusio*) is that Rome will mourn when Christ comes in judgment.

Another helpful text is Matthew 24:30, where these same two passages from Daniel 7 and Zechariah 12 are conflated to speak of the judgment coming upon Jerusalem in A.D. 70.

John says he is bearing witness to the word of God and the testimony of Jesus. What is the difference between the two?

This phrase "the word of God and the testimony of Jesus," or something like it, is used three more times in the book (1:9; 6:9; 20:4). The difference between the two appears to be that "the word of God" has reference to the general will of God, while "the testimony of Jesus" involves specific truths related to Christ. Revelation 12:17 is helpful in this regard as it tells us of those who "keep God's commands and hold fast to the testimony of Jesus" (NIV). It appears that instead of employing "the word of God" (as he does in other places), John uses "God's commands." This helps us to understand what's behind his use of the term.

LETTERS TO THE BATTLEFIELD

***"He who has an ear, let him hear what the Spirit says to the churches"* (2:7, 11, 17, 29; 3:6, 13, 22).**

The seven churches of Revelation 2-3 are addressed in just 51 verses, with Thyatira receiving the most attention with twelve verses. Flip through the rest of the New Testament, and you'll see this is far from normal. By comparison, other writers tend to linger over the communities and situations they address.

There's none of that in these Post-It® notes to the seven churches of Asia. These communities are facing critical situations. Those at Smyrna are about to suffer persecution, prison, and possible death (2:10), while Pergamum has already lost one of its members (2:13). Given these circumstances, it's not surprising that these messages have the brevity and terseness of battlefield directives. The churches are locked in a life and death struggle with certain aspects of their culture, some of their peers, false teachers, compromise, and apathy. They are in full battle mode.

Just as war produces heroes, traitors, casualties, and survivors, we find all of these present in the letters. Smyrna and Philadelphia are standing nobly, and the risen Christ has nothing but commendation for them. Laodicea occupies the other end of the spectrum. The remaining churches (Ephesus, Pergamum, Thyatira, and Sardis) have some definite work to do, but they aren't without their strengths either. In short, we find the full range of responses to the times in these churches. It's important to note this so that we'll appreciate that the rest of the book addresses all of these situations, not just those that were in need of deliverance.

How should we hear what the Spirit has to say to us today? Though we are far removed by time and place from these communities, the trials and temptations spoken of are not; they are very much with us. In parts of Africa, India, the Middle East, and other places, there is an increasing number of believers who face persecution and even death for following Christ. For disciples everywhere, there is always pressure to accommodate the teachings of Jesus (as well as our lifestyle) to our culture.

As critical as these might be, it seems that our greatest temptation is to live along the margins of discipleship rather than in the middle. It is the heresy that is fashioned around the notion that Jesus *rounds off* our life vs. Jesus *is* our life. As a result, we end up worshipping life rather than the God who gives it.

Whether we are living in the margins of love (2:4-5) or commitment (3:15-16), the periphery is a place where we lack the kind of vision and clarity we need (3:17). In battlefield terms, it is walking around taking pictures with our smart phone to post on social media rather than being at our respective posts, doing what needs to be done. In biblical terms, it is King David restlessly hanging around the palace rather than being out on the battlefield (2 Samuel 11:1). We may or may not survive; we may or may not fall into temptation, but the larger point is that we are incidental to what is going on around us. After all, the real question is not whether there is a battle going on, but whether we are spectators or participants.

QUESTIONS

1. What's different about the situation of the seven churches of Asia compared to other churches in the New Testament that received letters?
2. Do you think disciples today face persecution? Why or why not?
3. What do you think are some of the temptations that come when facing oppression? Do we see any evidence of these in the letters to the seven churches?

HOPE IS HARD WORK

"To the one who conquers..." (2:7, 11, 17, 26; 3:5, 12, 21).

None of the seven congregations to which John writes have precisely the same set of circumstances. Like any seven churches today, they share certain conditions and traits, but there are also unique aspects about their situations. The congregations in Ephesus and Pergamum are both challenged by a group known as the Nicolaitans (2:6, 15), but while Ephesus hates their practices (2:6), Pergamum has some who embrace them (2:15). Smyrna and Philadelphia are experiencing trouble from those who say they are Jews but in reality are of "the synagogue of Satan" (2:9; 3:9). Smyrna has more hardship and persecution ahead, but Philadelphia is going to be spared from "the hour of trial" (3:10).

Despite their differences, all are challenged to do the same thing: be victorious (NIV). If you have another translation, it might use "overcome" or "conquer," but all are told to do this at the closing of the message Jesus gives to each congregation (2:7, 11, 17, 26; 3:5; 12, 21). Near the end of Revelation, God speaks of the blessings that come to those who are victorious (21:7).

Since no church shares the same situation, being victorious works out differently for each group. For the disciples at Ephesus, it's repenting and doing the things they did at first (2:5). For Pergamum, it's renouncing the false teaching some are following (2:16). Smyrna must endure, and Philadelphia is to "hold on to what you have" (3:11 NIV). For all of these churches, overcoming is about remaining faithful to God regardless of what their situations might be.

Embedded in this charge to overcome are some important truths. One is that adversity is not omnipotent; Jesus is. No matter what the issue is (and these churches were facing significant ones), through Christ it can be conquered. Sins can be repented of and lives transformed. Hardships can be met with patient endurance. Faith in God is the full and final answer to every situation.

When we look at it this way, we see another reality; victory has to do with surrendering to God the things that are in our control. Christ didn't ask these disciples to stop all of the evil that was going on in the world, but He did command them to stand against its presence in their lives. Unlike athletic contests, business deals, and so much of life where there are often factors beyond our control, being faithful is about what lies within our control—fleshing out our faith on a daily basis.

All of this brings us back to hope. If adversity isn't omnipotent, and God doesn't require what we are unable to give, then we have every reason to have hope. This is critical because overcoming doesn't happen by accident; it is the result of having a strong and sustained sense of hope.

The final truth is the most overlooked; hope is hard work (or at least it should generate hard work). The Scripture speaks of "endurance inspired by hope" (1 Thessalonians 1:3 NIV). Overcoming is simply the patient, outworking of hope. It begins with Jesus and His victory and works its way through our lives.

And there's rarely anything "easy" about it.

QUESTIONS

1. What do you think of when you hear the word "victory"? In what sense does John use the word?
2. Several truths are connected to Jesus' charge to be victorious: 1) Adversity is not omnipotent; Jesus is, 2) Victory has to do with giving God what we can control, and 3) Before you can overcome, you must first have hope. Which of these is most important to you? Why?
3. How is hope hard work? Can you think of some examples?

THE SLEEPING DISCIPLES

***"Wake up, and strengthen what remains and is about to die, for I have not found your works complete in the sight of my God"* (3:2).**

The above is what Jesus said to a group of first-century disciples at Sardis (3:2). It's not the best news in the world, but it's not the worst. It's kind of a good news/bad news scenario. It says, "You were headed in the right direction, but you stopped. You need to get moving again and finish what you started."

For most people, if they've heard about any of the churches to which John writes in Revelation, it's Laodicea. They are the lukewarm church that Jesus wants to spit out of His mouth (3:15-16). I think Laodicea gets the lion's share of attention because their situation syncs with the apathy that is prevalent in our culture, as witnessed by many who profess Christ but make little or no effort to either learn or practice what He taught.

But I gravitate more toward Sardis and the situation there. For one thing, the situation there wasn't as simple. At Laodicea, everyone comes under Jesus' indictment. At Sardis, there are some who are "worthy" (v. 4). Then there are those who need to wake up (v. 2). This corresponds more to the situations I've experienced in the congregations of which I've been a part. From my perspective, I don't think of any of the groups as being lukewarm (although there were probably a few individuals who qualified). I think they were much more like Sardis in that there were some who were models for me, and then there were some who needed to be awakened so they could complete the things they had started.

In my earlier years (when I had of lots of zeal and not as much discernment), I usually relegated everyone who wasn't a model for me to the lukewarm category. With growth, I came to see how wrong this was. The truth was that while there were a few who were deserving of that designation, most weren't. They had noble intentions but had gotten bogged down in the mire of one thing or another and were now spinning their wheels. They were part of the community of faith because they cared and wanted something more, even if they didn't know exactly what it was or how to make it happen. I hadn't honored their intentions or their struggle.

I believe this describes many people in the kingdom today. For one reason or another, they've been spiritually shut down for so long that they've become numb to their situation. Their flame is on autopilot, and their hope has gone into hibernation. If something doesn't happen, they will go to their grave this way.

What needs to happen is they must come out of their coma. They must stop living in the past and finish what God has started. He has purposes for their lives that aren't being fulfilled. They need to rekindle their intimacy with Him so there can once more be urgency about their calling.

John didn't publish a sequel to Revelation, so we don't know what happened to the sleeping disciples at Sardis. I'd like to think they woke up before it was too late and experienced the joy of living all out for Jesus. Whatever else we do, let's make sure we don't miss out on that.

QUESTIONS

1. Describe the situation in the church at Sardis.
2. From 3:2-3, what is involved in sleeping disciples waking up?
3. Why are we sometimes tempted to live in the past?

WORTHY

"Yet you have still a few names in Sardis, people who have not soiled their garments, and they will walk with me in white, for they are worthy" **(3:4).**

When Jesus spoke to the church at Sardis, He did more than afflict the comforted; He also comforted the afflicted. There were a "few" there who were "worthy" (v. 4). They had not soiled their clothes, which in the context means they hadn't compromised their beliefs or their behavior as so many others had done.

We know people like this, don't we? No matter what the circumstances, they're going to do what's right. Whether it's easy or difficult, trendy or unpopular, instantly gratifying or requiring boatloads of patience, it makes no difference to them. They don't live this way because they have to, but because they want to. Their passion for God is what drives them to obey the unenforceable. No one has to light a fire under them; they inspire others by the way they live. They're not one of the faint or flickering stars; they beam brightly.

And we're blessed by such people. They pull us upward. They point out possibilities to us of what we could be as we grow and allow God to work more and more in our lives. As I write this, I'm thinking of two such people I've been blessed to know. They weren't perfect, but their faith was genuine, their love was true, and their lives made a difference. Both of them have graduated from this life, but their lives still speak.

Neither of these people did anything of headline significance. In fact, they would have been uncomfortable with attention being called to them or their deeds. They didn't wear t-shirts pointing to their involvement in this cause or that. You weren't going to see their names on placards at the local store saying they were donors to some charitable effort or see them on television helping to serve food to the homeless one day a year. No, their lives were characterized by a consistent consideration of others and the simple, quiet, everyday actions that go with it. They did the little things that received no attention but made all the difference.

One of the people I'm thinking of is Willis. He walked across the street one day to welcome a new neighbor. Not much to it, but it was exactly the kind of thing he was known for doing. It started a relationship that grew into friendship and resulted in the neighbor coming to Christ. At Willis' funeral, it was thrilling to hear this brother express his eternal gratitude for what started as a small kindness and grew into a life-saving relationship.

The sister I'm thinking of is Marlene. She was known for opening her home to all people, but especially younger people who were in that stage of life when they were trying to figure out who they were and what they wanted to do. She provided first-class nurturing and encouragement and affected the lives of many people, including mine, in immeasurable ways.

Both of these people had their share of difficulties and hard times, which they handled with courage and an optimism borne of their faith. I have been blessed and challenged by the Christ I saw in them.

And what of such people? After Jesus says they are worthy, He adds that others who overcome will be "like them" (v. 5 NIV)—dressed in white, have their names in the book of life—and be acknowledged by Jesus before the Father and His angels (3:5). The ones who are worth following in life are worth following in death!

QUESTIONS

1. In your words, what does it mean to be "worthy?"
2. Can you think of someone who belongs in this category? In what ways are they a model to others?
3. Should we put such people up on a pedestal, or simply be inspired by their character and maturity? What is the difference?

WHAT JESUS DIDN'T SAY

I think it's instructive to look at Jesus' words to the seven churches and think about what He doesn't say. After all, His words are relatively few and obviously deal with the most vital issues facing these communities. But how about what isn't mentioned? Is there something omitted that we thought would be there?

I imagine some are surprised to find that Jesus doesn't say something to the effect of, "I don't know where you got this church idea from, but it wasn't from Me—I'm all about spirituality, not organized religion." After all, the Jesus of the gospels doesn't appear to have been a member of any church; in fact, he was rejected by the synagogue he grew up in (Luke 4:14-30). Furthermore, His harshest words were reserved for some of the church-going establishment (Matthew 23). You would think there would be something about this in His messages to these churches.

But there's not.

What we see instead is Jesus standing among the churches and claiming them as His. And it's not a naïve ownership that He exercises. He sees them for all that they are: good, bad, and indifferent. He sees them as responsible for each other, so he doesn't address them as isolated individuals but as a congregation. I'm convinced that He also sees them for what they can become and understands that they won't be able to reach that by themselves. They'll need the strength that can come only through community.

Then there are some who are out of sorts that Jesus didn't say something in accordance with their (mis)understanding of grace. They seem to think God doesn't have any expectations for His children other than to forgive them for whatever they do, whenever they do it, no matter why they did it. But instead of saying something like "I love you and just want you to know that there's nothing you could ever do to disappoint Me," He says things like, "I will spit you out of My mouth" (3:16), and "If you do not repent, I will come to you and remove your lamp stand from its place" (2:5 NIV). This Jesus takes right living seriously and expects His followers to do so as well.

Finally, I suppose there are some who are bitterly disappointed that Jesus doesn't say something along the lines of, "I love you and would never allow you to suffer any kind of pain or hardship." Instead, He speaks of suffering and being faithful "even to the point of death" (2:10 NIV), and of a disciple named Antipas being put to death (2:13).

Add all of this up and what do you get? You get a Christ who creates community, a Jesus who will be Lord of all or not at all, and a Savior who understands that love and suffering are at times inseparable for Him and His. All of this reminds us that Christ calls us to be disciples, not dabblers.

But I think it tells us something more. It tells us that hope is much more than a good feeling about what is to come. It manifests itself in specific behaviors that reflect our faith in the future through Jesus (see 1 Thessalonians 5:6-8). Because we believe in what He did and will continue to do, we are committed to living for Him. Living in some other way, as many in these congregations were doing, is a repudiation of our true hope, which is anchored in Him.

Let's live with the hope of Christ.

QUESTIONS

1. Why is community so important for followers of Jesus? What Scriptures speak to the importance of community?
2. Which of the three things discussed in this section—community, living righteously, and experiencing hardship—do you think people struggle with the most? Which challenges you the most?

FAQ

What is the general background of the churches John is writing?

The place to begin is to recognize we're most interested in the background of these churches a few years after John writes Revelation. As we'll see when we get to Revelation 17, John is writing during the latter part of Vespasian's reign (sometime during the late 70s). The treacherous times Revelation speaks to will occur a few years later, during the rule of an eighth king, two emperors after Vespasian (17:10-11).

Vespasian rules from A.D. 69-79 and is succeeded by his son Titus who reigns for just two years. Upon Titus' death, Vespasian's other son, Domitian, comes to the throne in A.D. 81 and rules until his assassination in A.D. 96. We're interested in the background of these churches during Domitian's reign because that's when things became most difficult for these churches in Asia.

In regard to this period, it seems there are two extremes to avoid when thinking about the conditions of these congregations. One is over-emphasizing the role of the imperial cult (emperor worship) and making it the only lens through which we look at the book. The other extreme is to under-emphasize or dismiss it entirely and simply see the churches as oppressed or seduced by the Empire's malignant ways. I think the truth is somewhere between these two positions.

Rome certainly stands against God in many ways. Like Egypt, Assyria, and Babylon before it, it epitomizes the arrogant exercise of power. Corruption, violence, greed, immorality, and cruelty are written into its DNA. Compromise with Rome is not limited to saying, "Caesar is Lord" while offering a pinch of incense to a likeness of the emperor; it is embracing any of its godless values! This is one of the ways Revelation speaks so powerfully to us today.

That said, it is also clear from Revelation 13, 16-17, 19-20 that something more than general lawlessness is taking place in the province of Asia. In these chapters (especially Revelation 13, 17), John is given a detailed vision that has to do with an eighth king (emperor) who wages war against the Lamb and His followers (17:11-14; 13:7). This corresponds with a vision the prophet Daniel was given centuries before (Daniel 7). Coupled with the allusions to the imperial cult (13:4, 14-15; 14:9; 15:2; 16:2; 19:20; 20:4), it's compelling evidence pointing to a very specific historical context for the book; something that isn't happening before Domitian and doesn't happen after him because God puts an end to it.

What are some specific things happening in Asia during Domitian's reign?

The Imperial Cult. Let's start with the imperial cult. At the time of Revelation's writing, the cult is an increasingly important branch of the Roman religious tree. Wright calls it the fastest growing religion in the Empire, and Steven Friesen says in *Imperial Cults and the Apocalypse of John* that Asia was on "the cutting edge." The imperial cult plays a critical role in the veneration of the state and its many gods. It begins when Julius Caesar is deified upon his death and is later employed by Augustus and successive emperors to varying degrees. In Rome and Italy, an emperor is never worshipped while he is alive, but in outlying provinces like Asia, it's a different story.

The people of Asia have a history of worshipping their rulers that goes as far back as Alexander the Great, and they are heavily involved in the imperial cult. Three of the seven cities addressed in Revelation have built provincial temples in honor of different Roman emperors. Pergamum built a temple to Augustus. Smyrna competed with other cities and won the right to build a temple to Tiberius. (According to the first-century Roman senator and historian Tacitus, Laodicea and Sardis were two of the ten cities they competed against.) For the cities of Asia, this is a way of showing that although they are geographically distant from Rome, their allegiance is nonetheless strong. For their part, Rome encourages the imperial cult because it is a way of unifying the Empire.

The third provincial temple is the one that holds the most interest for us. Ephesus builds a temple to the Flavians (Vespasian, Titus, and Domitian) c. A.D. 90. It is often referred to as the Temple of the Sebastoi (i.e., venerated ones). Unlike the temples at Pergamum and Smyrna which also honor the Senate and Rome, the temple at Ephesus is dedicated exclusively to the emperors (Friesen), and reflects Domitian's popularity in the provinces (Brian Jones, *The Emperor Domitian*). Ephesus even initiates its own Olympic games in Domitian's honor, giving him the title Zeus Olympios (Friesen).

As the commercial center and largest city in the province, Ephesus now becomes the focal point for the imperial cult in Asia (Oster). The statue bases in the temple bear inscriptions from thirteen cities of Asia, displaying the province's solidarity with the city and temple (Friesen). This all has a tremendous impact upon the city's inhabitants.

Participation in the imperial cult doesn't appear to have been mandatory. It was more like showing up for work—no one is going to force you to do it, but if you fail to, there will be consequences. While there's no evidence of a systemic, empire-wide persecution of Christians by Domitian for refusing to participate in the imperial cult (or for any other reason), that doesn't mean there isn't anything extensive and localized occurring among the churches of Asia that rises to the level of what we see in Revelation. Yet it's probably best not to think of the consequences as coming from local officials (at least not initially) but from one's peers, since honoring the gods was a routine part of business, political, social, and athletic events (like saying the Pledge of Allegiance or singing the national anthem, but with more serious repercussions for non-involvement). Failure to participate probably affects disciples socially and economically at first, and escalates from there. The imperial cult then, as embodied in the Temple of the Sebastoi at Ephesus, casts an enormous shadow over the churches of these seven cities and would be one of the catalysts of the troubles addressed in Revelation.

Fiscus Judaicus. Unrelated to the imperial cult, but also associated with Domitian is the *Fiscus Judaicus.* After Jerusalem is destroyed by the Romans in A.D. 70, Vespasian imposes this tax upon the Jewish people. Sometime during Domitian's reign (Jones puts it at A.D. 85), he clamps down on the actual collection of the revenue. Many had been avoiding payment through various means (concealing their Jewish identity, denying their heritage, claiming to be apostates, etc.). Domitian is serious about putting an end to such evasive practices to the extent that the Roman historian Suetonius speaks of witnessing a scene where a ninety-year old man is publicly examined to see if he is circumcised!

In the eyes of Domitian, Christians are considered prime candidates for this tax since they do so many "Jewish" things—abstaining from fornication as well as meat sacrificed to idols, being "atheists" (Rome's word for those who don't participate in the imperial cult or worship the traditional gods), and following a god named Yahweh. Domitian's concern is revenue, not appreciating the differences between Jews and Christians. From this perspective, Christians are much more like Jews than unlike them.

Christians have some obvious issues with the tax. They don't consider themselves Jewish in terms of their primary identity and aren't welcome in the Jewish community since they embrace Jesus as the Messiah. Christ's references to the "synagogues of Satan" at Smyrna (2:9) and Philadelphia (3:9) show that there is a significant breach between the two communities. Furthermore, while Vespasian kept the tax at the same amount (half a shekel/two drachma) as the temple tax (Exodus 30:13; Matthew 17:24ff), he expanded its liability from males twenty to fifty years of age, to everyone: men, women, children, freedmen, and servants. This is a substantial burden for most families. Since Christians aren't part of the Jewish community and didn't participate in the uprising that resulted in the destruction of the city and brought about the tax, it's not difficult to see why they regard any attempt to apply the tax to them as unjust and oppressive.

Here's where the situation could become extreme for the church. If Jewish Christians don't pay the tax and are discovered (presumably through a physical examination like the one Suetonius refers to), they can be prosecuted for tax evasion and their property confiscated. Informants abound (they are paid a percentage of whatever is confiscated), so it's not difficult to imagine anyone, but especially people from the synagogue (hurt over the "defection" of believers from their group), extorting them or turning their names over to revenue officials.

The situation is even bleaker for Gentile Christians. While a physical exam might clear them of tax evasion, Marius Heemstra (*The Interpretation and Wider Context of Nerva's Fiscus Judaicus Sestertius*) suggests it is likely to be replaced with the charge of atheism. While the Romans are generally tolerant of the Jewish failure to support the traditional gods because it is an established tradition within a generally confined community, it is a different situation for those outside the Jewish community (i.e., Christians). They follow Someone crucified by Rome for insurrection, refer to Him as "Lord," and are committed to spreading His kingdom all over the world. In the politically-charged, revenue-hungry atmosphere of Domitian's reign, this is more than enough to qualify them for confiscation of their possessions or something worse.

Suetonius makes reference to Domitian seizing the property of the living and the dead in an effort to bolster revenues. Cassius Dio, a Roman historian who lived in the second and third century A.D. and wrote an eighty-volume history of Rome, speaks of people having their property confiscated due to their atheism. He also tells of Flavius Clemens, Domitian's cousin, and others being executed for the same reason. And while the *Fiscus Judaicus* is enforced throughout the empire, it's not hard to imagine the circumstances in Asia, heavy taxation (Jones) coupled with the eagerness to please Rome, creating especially intense conditions there. Heemstra's conclusion is that the situation under Domitian is so egregious (even by Roman standards) that the next emperor, Nerva, puts a halt to Domitian's excessive collection policy (limiting it to practicing Jews), and does away entirely with the practice of using *Fiscus Judaicus* to prosecute non-Jews for atheism.

All of this means that during Domitian's time, the followers of Jesus in Asia can come under tremendous scrutiny by local officials. Not paying the tax or honoring the nation's gods is a combination the Romans will find difficult to accept and leads to the circumstances we find described in Revelation.

Application to the seven churches. We see this tension created by the imperial cult, the Fiscus Judaicus, and the differing responses to them, in Jesus' messages to the churches. As Oster has pointed out, the references to Old Testament figures of Balaam and Jezebel in Christ's messages to Pergamum (2:14ff) and Thyatira respectively (2:20ff) have to do with accommodation. Just as these false prophets induced Israel to compromise their faith, so their counterparts in Thyatira and Pergamum were introducing the disciples to some sort of spiritual accommodation, conceivably as a way to lessen official scrutiny and pressure. This might involve some type of offering to a Roman god or emperor (13:14ff, 14:9ff). The Nicolaitans (2:6,15) probably belong in this category as well. Christ's commendation of the disciples at Smyrna despite suffering affliction and poverty (2:9) could be understood as His recognition of the financial loss that has occurred as a result of their refusal to honor the particular gods of a business guild or trade association. His condemnation of Laodicea and their material wealth (3:17) could be for their accommodation and embracing of such gods.

In conclusion, while we'll never know as much as we'd like to about what is specifically happening with these churches, our knowledge of the imperial cult and Fiscus Judaicus provides us with a good base to build upon in understanding the hardships faced by these seven churches.

What have we seen?

Times were tough for seven struggling churches in first-century Asia and about to become even more difficult. Rome's pagan presence loomed large over them. The risen Christ stands among the lampstands (churches) to assure them He is with them. He speaks through John to the churches, offering comfort, rebuke, warning, and promise according to their needs.

PART TWO

John Sees Heaven

The vision of John continues, but it moves from Patmos to heaven. He sees the throne of heaven occupied and the Lamb step forward to open the scroll revealing the future. What he sees and describes in these two chapters provides the context for the opening of the seals in Revelation 6, as well as furnishes the disciples with the bedrock assurance they will need for such a critical time.

The Holy, Creator God on the throne in heaven (4:1-11)
The Lamb Who was slain and the scroll (5:1-14)

THE THING WITH FEATHERS

"After this I looked, and behold, a door standing open in heaven!" (4:1).

The reclusive poet of Amherst, Emily Dickinson, penned these famous words about hope:

Hope is the thing with feathers
That perches in the soul
And sings the tune without the words
And never stops at all

And sweetest in the Gale is heard
And sore must be the storm
That could abash the little Bird
That kept so many warm

I've heard it in the chillest land
And on the strangest Sea
Yet never in Extremity,
It asked a crumb of me.

In Revelation 4:1, the symbol before us is not a bird, but an open door. But just as Dickinson's bird isn't just any bird, John's door isn't any door. It's one that is standing open in heaven!

Doors are about access. If a door is shut, entrance is denied. If it is open, it is an invitation to step through to whatever is on the other side. In this case, it is not a door to heaven but to what is going on in heaven. Specifically, it's about heaven's role in the immediate future (4:1; 1:1, 3).

As such, it's about access to the Father, Son, and Spirit. It's an inside look at what is happening on the throne that rules the universe. Just as Revelation 2-3 took John's audience past appearances to provide an intimate look at their churches, so John is now going to take them past all the speculation about heaven to show them what is really going on there relative to what was going to take place.

The open door then is a door of hope. It is exactly what John's readers need to see as they are about to go through their own chilling and strange times relative to Rome and Domitian. It is exactly what we need to see as well. As we step through it, our hearts will be assured, and our steps secured to live deeper, nobler, richer lives for the One who died and lives for us.

QUESTIONS

1. "Doors are about access." How is this true when we hear about doors in 3:8, 20?
2. How is the open door of 4:1 a door of hope?
3. Dickinson concludes her poem by saying that hope never asks anything of us. Do you think that's true? Why or why not?

OF COMFORT & COURAGE

"Day and night they never cease to say, 'Holy, holy, holy, is the Lord God Almighty, who was and is and is to come!'" (4:8).

"Oh say can you see..." are the familiar words that begin *The Star Spangled Banner*. They were written to express the joy of seeing the American flag still flying over Fort McHenry after an overnight assault by the British during the War of 1812. Francis Scott Key, the song's writer, had been negotiating a prisoner exchange with the British aboard one of their boats. When the battle broke out, he watched from the ship as the fort was bombarded. When it was over, he waited anxiously until daylight to see if the flag was still flying—and it was! The sight of the flag inspired the poem that was later set to music and became America's national anthem.

In much the same way, what John sees in Revelation 4-5 is meant to inspire disciples who are involved in a spiritual war. These two chapters form the introduction to a vision John receives of the immediate future (4:1). The scene is in heaven, and it assures John and his readers that no matter how chaotic things on earth might seem, God is in control. To that point, everything he sees is described in relationship to the throne, which is referred to twelve times in Revelation 4.

And just as the White House is more than a house that is white, the throne is more than the place where God resides; it speaks of power, authority, and dominion. Image-wise, we are being assured in no uncertain terms that it is not Caesar who is in charge, but God. There is a throne in heaven, and it's occupied!

And what of the One who sits upon the throne? What are we "told" about Him? Through a rich tapestry of images (much of it from the tabernacle/temple), we learn that the One who sits on the throne in heaven is nothing like the one who sits on the throne in Rome. He is holy! This is the constant message of the four creatures (v. 8).

Why the emphasis on God's holiness? Certainly one reason is to show the basis for the judgment that is about to be revealed against Rome (Bauckham). God's holy character has been violated by the wicked kingdom, and its time of reckoning is about to come.

God's holiness means more than this though. It offers comfort—not just by letting us know that the throne of heaven is occupied, but in assuring us that the power that rules the universe is righteous. The world has seen far too many nations and leaders abuse their authority to get excited about hearing that someone has power. No one celebrates when a country announces that it has developed nuclear capability—we all know where that inevitably leads. In the same way, John's disciples know all too well about Rome's power and how it is being used.

That's why, in this vision, we see God exalted not only for His power in creating everything (v. 11), but also for His holy character (v. 8). This message about God isn't just theology for learning, it's biography for living! Because God is all-powerful and all-good, the evil of Rome (or any other country) does not go unnoticed, and ultimately cannot be victorious. Knowing this makes a difference for the believer in the 21st century as it did for those in the first century.

Toward the end of the musical *Camelot,* King Arthur comes upon a young teenager named Tom. He has been stowed away in one of the boats that crossed the channel into France. He tells Arthur he wishes to become a Knight of the Round Table. The king is intrigued and wants to know where this desire came from. Was his village protected by a knight? Was his mother saved by a knight? Perhaps his father served a knight?

None of these, Tom tells him. He's heard the stories, "might for right and justice for all." Arthur's heard enough. He knights him "Tom of Warwick." His mission now is to return to England and share the story with others.

In this scene that John shows us, we see in the images and hear in the words the story of "might for right and justice for all." We've been knighted with comfort that we might live courageously for Christ and share His story with the world.

QUESTIONS

1. What is the significance of the word "throne" being repeatedly used by John? What does this say to us today?
2. How does God's holiness fit into the picture we see? Why is it comforting?
3. How can these things help us to live more courageous lives?

GOD'S HOLINESS & AN UNFLINCHING FAITH

"Day and night they never cease to say, 'Holy, holy, holy'" (4:8).

Because God is holy, so are His purposes. This is central to Revelation and must also be to us if we're to understand the book's message. Revelation is about much more than just "we win." That's true of course; it's just not enough. It's like meeting someone who tells you, "I made it." That's a truth that bears telling, but by itself it doesn't mean much. Did they make it through something substantial or trivial? It is the details of how and what they made it through that enrich those words and give them their meaning.

The truth of Revelation (and the larger story of Scripture) is we win, but we might be called upon to give our lives in the process, and we will almost certainly be called upon to suffer in some way at some point. That was the message the disciples heard in the first century (see Acts 14:21-22; 2 Timothy 3:12). It's an understatement to say that this isn't a message generally heard or embraced by believers today. Instead, we tend to equate "victory in Jesus" with the idea that we will never have to suffer. Listen to our prayers, and you'd think it was God's will that no follower of Jesus should ever have any pain.

But that's our will speaking, not God's. At a certain level, it's understandable—avoiding pain is instinctual. Accepting suffering is an act of trust. It is believing that there is a purpose for our pain, even if we're not able to fathom what it might be. It is a deep-seated conviction that God can use all of the circumstances of our life to His glory, even those circumstances we wouldn't choose for ourselves.

When we hear the four living creatures that are covered with eyes (so they don't miss anything, as we humans do), speak of God's holiness, they are not only confessing a character truth about Him, but a situational one as well. God is holy, and because He is, the oppression (and in some cases, martyrdom) that will come upon the churches of Asia (6:9-11) has a holy purpose. It is not accidental, incidental, or arbitrary.

This is a tough truth for those of us in the West. For disciples in other places (Nigeria, Pakistan, North Korea, etc.), it's a reality of life. If we're going to come to grips with the suffering we're called to (1 Peter 2:21ff, etc.), it begins with embracing both of these elements in the picture in Revelation 4. Not only is God on the throne, but it is the holy God who is in control. We can be assured that His purposes are not only beyond our understanding, but above it as well (Isaiah 55:8-9).

Revelation is as real as it gets. It was written to first-century brothers and sisters who were staring hardship, suffering, and death in the eye. John's message to them wasn't one of hand-wringing fear and despair, but heart strengthening hope: God and His purposes are holy; be faithful and the victory is yours. These are solid truths that produced the unflinching faith that is their legacy and our heritage.

QUESTIONS

1. How is it that the message of Revelation is more than just "we win"? Why is it important to understand this?
2. How is accepting suffering or hardship an act of trust in God?
3. Why do you think so many believers seem to be fixated with the idea that Christians should never suffer?

THAT'S THE WAY IT IS

"And he who sat there had the appearance of jasper and carnelian, and around the throne was a rainbow that had the appearance of an emerald" (4:3).

There's more good news in Revelation 4 relative to God's holiness. We see it in the rainbow that encircles the throne (v. 3). It isn't off to the side or pushed into the background; the rainbow so encompasses the throne that you cannot look at God without seeing it. The rainbow comes, of course, from the story of Noah and speaks to God's faithfulness (Genesis 9:12ff). It is the sign of the covenant He established with mankind and has honored ever since. The rainbow's presence in John's vision reminds us that we should not think of God without considering His great faithfulness.

The psalmist speaks of God's faithfulness being established in heaven (Psalm 89:2). That's fundamental because in the end, everything depends upon that. If God is not faithful, then we have no hope; it's as simple as that. His fidelity is the ground beneath our feet, and without it we have nothing to stand upon.

One of the first jobs I had was at a Western Auto store when I was in the ninth grade. I worked all day Saturday and after school during the week until the store closed, which was at 6:00 pm. The minutes before closing time inevitably found us standing at the front of the store in anticipation of a last-minute customer. One of the big color console televisions would be on and tuned in to the CBS news with Walter Cronkite. When the broadcast ended at 6:00, Cronkite would close by sonorously announcing, "And that's the way it is." Mr. Anderson, the owner of the store, would say, "That's the way it is, gentlemen." He would set the alarm, and we would head home. Long before "it is what it is," there was "that's the way it is."

God is faithful, and that's the way it is. The 24 elders around the throne clearly represent the people of God. As Jesus is both king and priest, so His followers are "a kingdom and priests" (1:6; 5:9-10 NIV). Their royal aspect (1 Peter 2:9) is evidenced by the crowns and thrones, while the priestly element is witnessed by the harps and offering of incense (5:8). Since the priestly function is in view here, and so much of the overall picture comes from the tabernacle/temple, the number 24 possibly comes from the divisions of the priesthood that were made by David in 1 Chronicles 24 (Jim McGuiggan, *The Book of Revelation*). But the truth we must not lose sight of is that we are and remain these things because God through Christ has "made us to be" them (1:6). We're right back to God's faithfulness.

It is imperative to our spiritual survival that we not become preoccupied with charting the rise and fall of our own devotion or that of others. If we do, chances are we will be disappointed, even discouraged. A better course is to do what John does here and focus on the One who sits on the throne and the profound truth of His radical reliability. We're better served by a rainbow than shifting sand.

That's the way it is.

QUESTIONS

1. Where does John tell us the rainbow is relative to the throne of God? What does this mean?
2. What is the connection between our hope and our Father's faithfulness? How is this important to our spiritual survival?
3. What kinds of things can we do to keep our focus on God rather than ourselves?

WORTHY IS THE LAMB

"Worthy are you to take the scroll and to open its seals, for you were slain, and by your blood you ransomed people for God from every tribe and language and people and nation" **(5:9).**

The message of Revelation 5 is one that awakens and inspires. It begins with John seeing a scroll in God's hand that is covered with writing containing important information pertaining to the future (cf. 5:1; 4:1). However, the scroll is secured with seven seals, and there is no one in heaven or on earth who is worthy to open it so that its contents can be revealed. John weeps because he recognizes the importance of the message for the people of God. There is the tantalizing sense of being so close and yet so far away.

The situation would have remained hopeless, but John hears that there is One who is worthy—the Lion from the tribe of Judah and the Root of David. These titles speak of power and majesty. We're told that He has "triumphed." This is why He is worthy (v. 4). Revelation (as well as the rest of the New Testament) emphasizes not only who Jesus was (God in the flesh), but also what He became as a man—how He alone offered perfect obedience to His Father (Philippians 2:5-11). This was His triumph and why He alone is worthy. And the more closely you look at Him (as John does here), the more clearly you see this truth.

Then something quite interesting occurs. Although Jesus is spoken of as a lion, what John sees is a lamb! Of course, it's not just any lamb. It's a lamb looking like it has been slain (because it has), but nonetheless, it's standing. But the lamb's not just standing; it's standing in the center of the throne (v. 6 NIV). If that's not enough, it also has seven eyes and seven horns. Got all of that?

In many ways, this picture is the ultimate symbol of Revelation. All of the important themes of the book are embedded in it. Paradox abounds: a lion that has the appearance of a lamb, life and death, vulnerability, omniscience (seven eyes), and omnipotence (seven horns). There is sacrificial love. There is an occupied throne. And there is victory and worthiness.

A lot of dark days in the history of mankind have been changed when people looked around as John did and saw that in midst of all of the broken lives and shattered spirits, there was Someone who was worthy—worthy of their hopes and dreams, of all that they cherished and held dear, of their lives, and even their deaths. No wonder all of heaven and earth worship Him (vv. 13-14).

Worthy is more than a word. It's more than who Jesus is as the Son of God. It's who He was as a human, as one of us, as One who came to this scarred planet. Not only did He leave as sinless as He came, but He brought truth, peace, healing, and hope like no one before or after. And for all of this He was put to death in the prime of His life by people like you and me who didn't understand. But now we can. By the grace of God we can see that all that is good, true, right, noble, lovely, and pure resides in Him. We can join the voices in proclaiming, "Worthy is the Lamb!"

QUESTIONS

1. Why is no one worthy to open the scroll? How is Jesus worthy? How is His worthiness different from what is mentioned in 3:4?
2. What are we told about the Lamb? What is significant about the way He is described?

FAQ

What is the sea of glass, and what is its significance?

The "sea of glass" that is in front of the throne refers to the basin that the priests used for washing their hands and feet prior to entering the tabernacle (Exodus 30:17-21). Failure to do so resulted in death (v. 20). This basin is referred to as "the sea" in Solomon's temple (2 Chronicles 4:2). Because the sea physically and ritually stood between the priests and entrance into the tabernacle/temple (i.e., God's presence in the Most Holy Place), it was a reminder of His holiness/separation from man. The thunder and lightning reminiscent of Sinai (Exodus 19:16ff), and the seven blazing lamps (which speak of the Holy Spirit), reinforce this as well.

What are the four living creatures, and what do they represent?

These are the cherubim. Far from being the cute, chubby-cheeked images we think of today, they are fearsome, other-worldly beings. The cherubim John sees here most closely resemble those spoken of in Ezekiel 1 and 10. Images of cherubim were woven into the curtain separating the Holy Place from the Most Holy Place in the tabernacle (Exodus 26:31ff). Inside the Most Holy Place, they were part of the atonement cover atop the Ark of the Covenant and looked down toward the tablets of law inside (25:18-20). In Solomon's temple, the cherubim had an even greater presence (1 Kings 6:29). They dominated the most holy place as they stood fifteen feet high, with their wings spanning the width of the room (vv. 23-28). A common thread in all of these occurrences is that the cherubim are close to God and, as such, bear witness to His holiness and majesty as they do in this vision.

Is God really in control of all things?

If He isn't in control, then who is? Philosophically, I don't think we have a lot of choices, and biblically speaking, I don't think we have any—God is in control. He always has been, and He always will be.

But how could He be in control when disciples were being oppressed, persecuted, and even put to death? The short answer is, the same way He was in control when His Son was crucified. We must come to grips with the fact that our Father's overarching purpose is to redeem humanity, not anesthetize us with a stream of unending pleasantries. Things happen which, from our limited perspective, appear wrong, cruel, and heartless. But like defibrillator shocks or radiation treatments, they are designed to bring life. I understand that all of this runs counter to our sensibilities, but maybe we ought to consider whether our sensibilities run counter to God.

What have we seen?

We've seen what we needed to see—the Father and the Son! We've seen that a holy God occupies the throne so we know that, no matter what it looks like, neither Rome nor anyone else on earth has the final word. Heaven does. And the Lamb who was slain stands at the center of the throne to reveal to the disciples what is to come. That's assurance!

PART THREE

A Look into the Future

With this section, we begin the part of Revelation that is most challenging because it is the least familiar. The Lamb begins to open the scroll by removing the seven seals. I think there's something to the suggestion that the opening of the seals is not the same thing as the revealing of the scroll (Bauckham). Even though we're in a book that defies convention, it makes sense that it would be difficult to begin reading a scroll until all seven seals were removed. Therefore, what we see in these chapters is preliminary to the actual revealing of the scroll in Revelation 11.

The first six seals (6:1-17)
The sealed and the multitude (7:1-17)
Seal seven (8:1)

THE RIDER ON THE WHITE HORSE

"Now I watched when the Lamb opened one of the seven seals, and I heard one of the four living creatures say with a voice like thunder, 'Come!' And I looked, and behold, a white horse! And its rider had a bow, and a crown was given to him, and he came out conquering, and to conquer" (6:1-2).

One truth to keep in mind while working through Revelation is that while there is something of a linear progression to the book (as seen in the movement from the seals to trumpets to bowls), much of its development is less straightforward. Instead, Revelation is more like one of those narrative murals you see in a museum or the rotunda of a historic building that have lots of different things going on at the same time. The difference is that, while the murals usually develop different parts of a story chronologically, John tends to tell the same story from different vantage points. This means we shouldn't always expect one truth to build upon the previous one. Though there is some of that, after Revelation 5, the book isn't written that way. Instead, truths swirl around in powerful but less predictable fashion. We're not as familiar or comfortable with this, but it's the way the prophets tended to write. And whatever else Revelation might be, John repeatedly tells us it is a prophecy (1:3; 19:10; 22:7, 10, 18-19).

All of this begins in Revelation 6 where six of the seven seals are opened, and what is revealed is in many ways like the preview of a movie. We see Jesus (seal 1), an army of three (seals 2-4), those who've suffered martyrdom at the hands of Rome (seal 5), and judgment upon Rome for the oppression of God's people (seal 6).

Seal 1	Rider on a white horse (Jesus)	6:2
Seals 2-4	Riders on red, black, and pale horses	6:3-8
Seal 5	Martyrs	6:9-11
Seal 6	Destruction of the world of the ungodly	6:12-17

While Revelation is about more than just these four things, they do encapsulate some major truths that will be repeated throughout John's vision.

In turning our attention to the first seal, we see the rider on the white horse is holding a bow and is almost certainly modeled after a Parthian warrior. The Parthians were renowned for archery in general, but especially their mounted archers. Cassius Dio tells us, "They practise from boyhood, and the climate and the land combine to aid both horsemanship and archery." Coins, artwork, and figurines depicting archers on horseback were common in Parthia.

The Parthians were a constant thorn in the side of Rome from a century before John wrote to a century afterwards. From Crassus' devastating defeat at Carrhae (53 B.C.), to Mark Antony's failed campaign into Parthia (37 B.C.), to Volgases IV's capture of Armenia (A.D. 161), the Parthians spelled trouble for Rome. Nearest to the time of John's writing was the war of A.D. 58-63, which saw the Roman general Paetus forced to surrender to the Parthians. According to Tacitus, the terms of surrender included vacating their forts in the area, and building a bridge over which the Parthian ruler paraded in triumph on an elephant, while the Romans, stripped of their possessions and weapons, passed under a yoke.

Implicit in this picture is the idea of someone that Rome is not able to handle. That someone is Jesus. In 19:11ff, we have the same rider appearing again, thereby bracketing John's vision of judgment with the triumphant Christ.

There's much encouragement here. The saints weren't able to deal with the power and policies of Rome (think of Paul's imprisonments, the Fiscus Judaicus, imperial cult, etc.), but their Lord could! Rome was no more able to handle Jesus at the time of the writing of Revelation than it could when they crucified Him and three days later He was back from the dead. At its start and finish, the vision John sees is punctuated by the triumphant rider on the white horse.

There are plenty of things that seem to tower over us: temptations, doubts and fears, mediocrity—the list goes on. These things can appear endless and threaten to grind us and our loved ones into dust. At such times, we would do well to remember that Jesus has dominion over all of these things (Colossians 1:15ff). And while no one gets immunity from tough times, we need to bracket them all with the rider on the white horse. He is what sustains our hope!

QUESTIONS

1. What major truths of Revelation are pictured in the first six seals?
2. Who were the Parthians, and what was their importance?
3. What reasons are there for identifying the rider of the white horse as Jesus? Do we see Jesus in the triumphant way He is presented here?

THE LAMB & A TRIO OF JUDGMENT, PART 1

"They were given authority over a fourth of the earth, to kill with sword and with famine and with pestilence and by wild beasts of the earth" (6:8).

If Jesus is the rider on the white horse, what do the other three horses represent? Do they have anything to do with Him? The answer is yes and no. Since they're all on horses, and they're all called out by one of the four living creatures (cherubim), it's obvious they are a unit in some sense. But as we'll see, there is an important distinction as well.

The horsemen, with their different appearances and functions, are drawn primarily from two different Old Testament books: Zechariah (1:7-11; 6:1-8) and Ezekiel (14:12-23). In Zechariah, the horses and their riders are presented as agents who patrol the earth for God and work behind the scenes to bring about His will. I think that's quite similar to the way they're presented here (although John describes them in greater detail and gives more attention to their actions). However, his use of the Ezekiel text is less straightforward.

In Ezekiel 14:12ff, God is speaking to the prophet about the judgment He is about to bring upon Jerusalem (v. 21). Four different scenarios are presented to Ezekiel. In each instance, a country's unfaithfulness has reached the point of provoking the judgment of God. Things are so bad in these situations that even the presence of Noah, Daniel, and Job wouldn't make a difference (v. 14). In each circumstance, the means of judgment is different—famine, beast, sword, and plague (vv. 12-20). God concludes his case against Jerusalem by telling Ezekiel their wickedness is so great that He is going to bring all of these against the city (v. 21). This was fulfilled when Nebuchadnezzar and the Babylonians razed Jerusalem in 586 B.C.

Following McGuiggan, I think John is borrowing from this in Revelation 6, but it is equally obvious that he adapts it for his purposes. For example, the four dreadful judgments are compressed to three of the horses, rather than the four we would expect. The second horse is obviously the sword, the third is famine, and the fourth is plague and beast. While "beast" isn't specifically used with the fourth horse, the fact that it is mentioned in v. 8, and spoken of after plague, suggests we are to understand it as embedded in the fourth horse.

Ezekiel 14:12-23 **Four Horsemen**	**Revelation 6:3-8** **Three Horsemen**
Famine (vv. 12-14)	Black horse (vv. 5-6)
Beasts (vv. 15-16	Pale horse (vv. 7-8)
Sword (vv. 17-18)	Red horse (vv. 3-4)
Plague (vv. 19-20)	Pale horse (vv. 7-8)

Why does John change things and have the four judgments compressed into three horsemen? As we've already noted, the rider of the first (white) horse is Jesus. Though the four riders are a unit (all are agents of God), Jesus is to be distinguished from the other three. Having triumphed over death, He wears the crown (*stephanos*), given to the victor and goes out as "a conqueror bent on conquest" (v. 2 NIV). But His conquest brings life, not judgment (John 3:17-18).

What of those who will oppose Him and persecute His followers? That's where the other three horsemen and the four dreadful judgments come in.

Jesus is sovereign; all things belong to Him, including death and Hades (1:18). The three horses that follow Him represent God's judgment upon those opposing the reign of Christ by persecuting His disciples (Acts 9:1-5). In this case, it is not Jerusalem, but Rome and Domitian. In response, a trio of judgments are sent against them. But note that as with many of God's judgments, these are partial (vv. 6, 8) with the intent of producing repentance.

By way of review, we've seen four of the seals removed, and they have provided us with two previews of what is to come. The first is that Christ, the Rider on the white horse, is out front and in control of all that will happen. The second is that Rome is going to suffer because of its oppression of the followers of Jesus. This judgment is aimed at repentance and will be fully developed in the seven trumpets in 8:2-11:19.

QUESTIONS

1. What do the other three horsemen represent? How is the first rider (Jesus) different from them? How are they related?
2. What does it mean to say that Jesus came to save, rather than condemn? How should this apply to His followers?

THE LAMB & A TRIO OF JUDGMENT, PART 2

"They were given authority over a fourth of the earth, to kill with sword and with famine and with pestilence and by wild beasts of the earth" (6:8).

While it's tempting to want to scour late first-century historical sources to find instances of sword, famine, plague, and beasts in order to show the fulfillment of this vision, that's not the way Revelation works. Even though the words found a more literal fulfillment in Ezekiel's time, I don't think we are to understand them here in such a way. As McGuiggan notes, John will say in 22:18 that anyone who adds to what he has written will have the plagues added to them.

Plagues are mentioned in eight different chapters of Revelation. They include things such as smoke, fire, sulfur proceeding out of the mouths of horses with heads like lions and tails like snakes (9:17-19), one-hundred-pound hailstones falling from the sky (16:21), and "every kind of plague" (11:6). Is John asking us to understand that all of these things will literally happen to those who distort the word (even today), or is he using a graphic metaphor that grabs our attention to let us know that they'll be subject to the wrath of God? In light of what John has already told us about how this vision has been communicated to him (page 35ff), the latter makes much more sense. In the same way, we are better off understanding the things brought by the horsemen as symbolic of what God will bring upon the unrighteous in an effort to move them to repentance. Either way, we need to decide how we're going to handle passages such as this because many more are on the way!

The idea of the gentle Jesus being followed by a trio of judgment is disturbing to some, but it shouldn't be. To those who submit to Him, Jesus is gentle as a lamb, but to those who rebel against Him and oppose His followers, He can be a lion. Our cultural sensitivities being what they are, we may not appreciate this, but to those Christians who lived with the reality of seeing their loved ones suffer and die due to persecution (see 6:9-11), these words offered profound comfort and assurance. We'll be much better off empathizing with the plight of our first-century family than feeling a need to apologize for God.

QUESTIONS

1. Are the things the horsemen bring meant to be understood literally? Why or why not?
2. Does Revelation challenge our view of Jesus? In what ways?

NOT FORGOTTEN

"When he opened the fifth seal, I saw under the altar the souls of those who had been slain for the word of God and for the witness they had borne. They cried out with a loud voice, 'O Sovereign Lord, holy and true, how long before you will judge and avenge our blood on those who dwell on the earth?'" (6:9-10).

Death removes us from the world of the living. Loved ones remain, and we leave. Their lives continue, while ours is over. We can gain some consolation if we know we'll be remembered—that we'll "live on" in the lives of others.

To be remembered is important. Birthdays, anniversaries, Mother's Day, and Father's Day all speak to the value we place on remembrance. Whatever else is true of those who had lost their lives due to holding to the word of God and the testimony about Jesus (vv. 9-11), they had not been forgotten.

They're given a robe (see 3:4) and told to wait a little longer. Their suffering and death have been noted by God, and those responsible will answer to Him. In essence, what they are being told is that they are being remembered. God hasn't forgotten them.

The writer of Hebrews speaks to this concern when he writes, "God is not unjust so as to overlook your work and the love that you have shown for his name in serving the saints, as you still do" (6:10). We're told that God "remembered" Noah after he and his family had been in the ark for 150 days (Genesis 8:1). Appearances may suggest otherwise, but they are always wrong. God remembers.

But He does more than remember those who are no longer with us, the time of their transition is important to Him as well. "Precious in the sight of the LORD is the death of his saints" (Psalm 116:15). In the story of Lazarus and the rich man, Lazarus is carried by angels to paradise (Luke 16:22). All of it matters to Him, and there's nothing about leaving this life that isn't in His hands.

Death changes nothing concerning God's commitment to us. He remembers us and acts for us in death just as He does in life. This is brought out by the fact that we're not told of others pleading for justice for those slain—it's the dead themselves who speak. And they are heard! For followers of the Lamb, there is hope in life and in death.

There are lots of questions we have about death and dying that we have no answers for. I suppose it would be nice to know those things, but then too, they might distract us from the few big truths we are given. The biggest truth is that Jesus holds the keys to death and Hades (1:18). Everything else is detail.

Write it down: we are not forgotten!

QUESTIONS

1. Why is it important to be remembered? Do you think this is a concern all people share?
2. How does John tell us those who were put to death due to their faith were being remembered?
3. What difference should being remembered by God make in our lives?

FAQ

Could the rider of the white horse be a symbol for the general conquest that takes place in the world?

This is a view popularized by some recent works on Revelation. It treats the four horseman as a unit without any distinctions by regarding them all as forces of evil at work in the world (i.e., either simply as an expression of man's wickedness, or as something allowed by God as a consequence of sin).

It's not clear to me in this view how the first rider (conquest) significantly differs from the second rider (war). This interpretation also doesn't take into account John's compression of the four plagues into the last three riders, something that is completely unnecessary if the four riders are a homogeneous unit, and each rider could simply represent a plague.

The biggest issue with this position is that the rider on the white horse not only becomes something other than Jesus; he is understood as being part of the evil that is inflicted/allowed on the earth. This goes against the way "white" is used throughout Revelation (McGuiggan). It occurs sixteen other times in the book and never in reference to evil. If the suggestion is made that white is used for the first rider to show how evil often appears as good (i.e., wars being justified to appear as good), and that this fits in with other parodies in the book (the beast being worshipped, appearing to be resurrected, appearing to be all powerful, etc.), then what is the purpose of the Parthian imagery? Its presence makes the rider anti-Roman (which in the book's context makes it an instrument of good, not evil).

In the end, a stronger case can be made that Jesus begins and ends the vision, that He is the One portrayed as being in charge of everything that happens. This is more consistent with the overarching message of the book.

Isn't the fourth horse/rider said to kill through sword, famine, plague, and wild beasts—rather than the second and third riders?

While that's correct, it's also true that the second and third riders are clearly aligned with the sword and famine. What's the solution? All three horses and riders are working together toward the same end, with Death and Hades in charge. Verse 8 speaks of them having "power." What is done by the other riders is done by them.

Isn't the sixth seal (6:12-17) referring to the end of the world?

Revelation 6:12-17 is one of those passages that, if you just opened your Bible to this text and started reading, it certainly sounds like the end of the world. Unfortunately, this is exactly the way this passage (and others in Revelation) are often approached. "See," someone will say, "It says what it means, and it means what it says." Or, "you don't need a commentary to understand what John is saying here. " While the spirit of taking God at His word is commendable, the assumption that you can jump into the middle of any conversation and understand exactly what is being said leaves something to be desired.

The truth is, if we understand the text literally, it leads to a contradiction. Verse 14 tells us that as a result of the great quake, "every mountain and island was removed from its place." If we take that literally, then this happened to every mountain and island—there were none left. That's a problem because, in v. 15, the people hide "in the caves and among the rocks of the mountains," while in v. 16, they called "to the mountains and rocks" to fall on them and hide them from the wrath of the Lamb.

What is John telling us with these words? Remember, these verses tell us what John sees when the sixth seal is opened. The first seal shows us the spread of Jesus' kingdom. The next three seals (representing sword, famine, plague, and wild beasts) have to do with partial judgment against Rome's kingdom because of its opposition to the kingdom of Christ. The fifth seal showed us those who had suffered at the hands of Rome. They asked God how long until justice is brought against the wicked and were told to wait just "a little longer" (v. 11). The sixth seal is meant to preview the beginning of an ultimate wrath against the wicked in response to the plea of the martyrs and Rome's impenitence. This judgment will be fully developed by the bowls of wrath in Revelation 16.

The language here is used frequently throughout Scripture, especially by the prophets of the Old Testament (see Isaiah 13:1, 9-10, 13; 34:9-10; Nahum 1:1, 5-6; Zephaniah 1:1-4). If you look at the context of these passages, none of them are meant to be understood literally. What they do mean is that God is destroying the "world" of the wicked—whether it is the world of the Babylonians, Judeans, Edomites, or whoever is opposing God.

SOMETHING WORTH CELEBRATING

"Do not harm the earth or the sea or the trees, until we have sealed the servants of our God on their foreheads." And I heard the number of the sealed, 144,000, sealed from every tribe of the sons of Israel" (7:3-4).

So far in John's vision, we've seen heaven open and God seated on the throne. We've seen the worthy Christ come forward and open six of the seven seals on the scroll, with the sixth seal revealing a staggering judgment that was to come against Rome. The seventh chapter is like pressing "pause." Instead of continuing to the seventh seal, our attention is directed to the followers of Jesus—we know judgment is coming upon Rome, but what happens to them? As others have pointed out, the textual connection for this is the question the wicked ask as the wrath of God and the Lamb comes upon them, "For the great day of their wrath has come, and who can stand?" (6:17).

The answer is given in two parts. First, we see the righteous sealed (vv. 1-8). Then we're taken back to the throne of God, where we see them in celebration and worship (vv. 9-17). They have "come out" of the great tribulation (v. 14 NIV). In all of this, we're to see the great contrast between those who follow the Lamb and those who don't.

To seal something is to protect it. Think about how we use a finish to seal a floor, table, or some other piece of furniture. Jesus' tomb was sealed by the Roman soldiers to make sure no one tried to break into it to steal His body (Matthew 27:65-66).

Many writers see Ezekiel 9 as providing the model for the sealing of the righteous. In Ezekiel 8, the prophet is given a vision that shows how widespread and intense idolatry is throughout Jerusalem. In Ezekiel 9, he sees a man whose mission is to put a mark on the forehead of "those who grieve and lament over all of the detestable things" that are being done in the city (v. 4 NIV). Six armed men follow him and put to death everyone who doesn't have the mark (9:5-6). This represents the judgment of Nebuchadnezzar and the Babylonians we saw earlier in Ezekiel 14. Those with the mark are exempt from this judgment.

This is the same thing that is going on in John's vision of 7:1-8. Before judgment comes, the righteous are to be sealed (v. 3). Of course, we're not to understand the sealing as literal any more than the number or ethnicity of those sealed (144,000 Jewish people) is to be taken literally. This is clear for several reasons. First, John has told us that we're in a book of signs. Furthermore, a literal understanding would require us to hold that there were no Gentile Christians (which is obviously incorrect), and that the Jewish Christians somehow amazingly consisted of exactly twelve thousand from each tribe! It's much better to see the 144,000 as a number representing completeness (12 x 12 x 1,000—all numbers that suggest totality or wholeness). Since the twelve tribes represent the people of God under the old covenant, the picture is telling us that no disciple is going to suffer from the judgment that comes against Rome.

Having said that, we need to note quickly that this is quite different from saying that no disciple is going to suffer. Indeed, Ezekiel 21:1-5 lets us know that when Jerusalem was destroyed by Nebuchadnezzar, righteous people died along with the unrighteous (McGuiggan). If they died the same as the unrighteous did, then what was the point of the marking? What difference did it make?

The answer is, all of the difference in the world! The unrighteous died as punishment for their wickedness; the righteous died in service to their Father. That's the difference between dying unblessed vs. blessed (Revelation 14:13).

Something of vital importance is being said about appearance vs. reality (another important theme of the book). When the righteous suffer and die along with the wicked, it appears to all the world that there is no difference between the two (Ecclesiastes 9:1ff). But the reality is that there is a tremendous difference. The wicked are being punished, and the righteous are not. Their death doesn't mean disfavor or dishonor; it is a sacrifice to their Father.

As noted earlier, this is a tough truth for people in Western culture to accept. Yet when all is said and done, our time here on earth isn't ultimately about avoiding suffering or death—it's about having life with God. At least that's what three young Hebrew men thought (Daniel 3:16-18). It was also true for those who overcame (Revelation 12:11). And in our better moments, it's what we know in our heart of hearts to be right. That's what John wants his readers to see. Whether they live or die, they have life with God!

That's something worth celebrating.

QUESTIONS

1. Who are the 144,000, and why are they sealed?
2. Does the sealing guarantee their physical safety? What should we learn from this?

BEFORE THE THRONE

"After this I looked, and behold, a great multitude that no one could number, from every nation, from all tribes and peoples and languages, standing before the throne and before the Lamb, clothed in white robes, with palm branches in their hands" (7:9).

There are multiple worship scenes in heaven throughout Revelation (chapters 4-5, 7, 11, 14-15, 19), and anyone who spends much time in the book recognizes they are an integral part of its structure. These scenes serve several purposes: they underscore the central conflict between the kingdom of God and the kingdom of Rome, they act as a counterpoint to the chaos and hostility on earth, and they call those who read to a deeper celebration, joy, and reverence for God and the Lamb and away from the idolatry of any kind.

The scene in 7:9-17 involves the same group of people that have been sealed in vv. 1-8. Whereas they were previously spoken of as 144,000 Jewish people, they are now identified as "a great multitude that no one could count, from every nation, tribe, people and language" (v. 9 NIV). If we're correct in understanding the 144,000 Jewish people as representative of the totality of God's people, then they would be a great multitude that included people from all backgrounds. So it is the same group being viewed from a different perspective.

This understanding is corroborated when we read that the multitude has "come out of the great tribulation" (v. 14 NIV). Since we've just seen the 144,000 sealed before harm comes to the world (7:4; 6:12-17), we either have to conclude that the two groups are the same, or that John describes one group, then without any explanation drops them and moves on to a second group.

This determination is important because seeing the 144,000 and the multitude as a single group unifies the two parts of John's vision (marked by the "after this I saw/after this I looked," vv. 1, 9). While the sealing in the first part of the vision is significant, it is incomplete without the scene before the throne. The sealing tells us they were protected through the tribulation (though not necessarily from it, as we have discussed), but showing them in worship before the throne completes the picture.

After all, what do those who have been delivered do? They praise God! They speak "with a loud voice" (v. 10) of the One who brought them salvation. This scene is modeled after the Feast of Tabernacles (Leviticus 23:33-43). The feast occurred five days after the Day of Atonement when the nation was purged of its sin and after they had gathered the harvest. Israel was to "celebrate" (v. 41) and "rejoice before the Lord" (v. 40). Those who have had their robes washed in the blood of the Lamb and have been part of His harvest know the joy and celebration of the feast.

For those who belong to Christ, this is our story as well.

QUESTIONS

1. Who is the great multitude that is spoken of? What are some reasons for identifying them with the 144,000?
2. Why do the scenes of sealing and worship belong together? How does this relate to our worship?

FAQ

What are the four winds of the earth?

Wind is used throughout Scripture in connection with the activity of God. As such, it is invisible, powerful, and mysterious (John 3:8). It is wind that causes the flood waters to recede (Genesis 8:1), and the waters of the Red Sea to part (Exodus 14:21). In Daniel 7, it is "the four winds of heaven" (v. 2) that churn up the sea and cause four kingdoms to arise. In Revelation 7:1-3, it is the activity of God relative to the judgment He is sending upon Rome. In the vision John sees, it is temporarily suspended so that the righteous might be marked out. In all of this, we are to see that God is in total control—of judgment, of marking, of everything!

Why are Dan and Ephraim not included in the twelve tribes in 7:5-8?

It's rarely an easy matter to say why something is omitted from any biblical list, unless the writer sees fit to tell us! For that matter, why are Levi and Joseph on the list? Some have suggested that it has to do with the fact that Jeroboam established altars for calf worship and introduced his own priesthood at Bethel (in Ephraim) and Dan (1 Kings 12:25ff). This was obviously a critical point in the overall movement of Israel away from God. When you combine this with the fact that the congregations John writes to are struggling against the many forms of paganism present in Roman culture, it makes sense that he leaves Ephraim and Dan off the list of the redeemed because of their association with idolatry. Having said that, note that while the tribe of Dan is functionally left off the list, Ephraim is omitted only in name. With Joseph (Ephraim's father) added to the list along with Joseph's other son, Manasseh, the tribe of Joseph becomes just another way of referring to Ephraim.

How can something be made white by being washed in blood (7:14)?

This is just one of many paradoxes in Revelation: the Lion that is a Lamb, the Lamb that is slain yet standing, wealth that is poverty, poverty that is wealth, a wilderness where life is sustained, etc. One of the major truths we're to take away from all of this is that we're not to put too much trust in the way things seem. Rather than be tyrannized by appearances, we should place our faith in the extraordinary power of God and the Lamb.

What have we seen?

We've seen the seven seals removed and the preview they furnish us of what is to come when the scroll is revealed. In that preview, a victorious Jesus on a white horse is out in front of everything. We've also heard of the saints' martyrdom and Rome's judgment. Special assurance has been given to disciples in the marking of the 144,000. It won't hurt us to remember that the seals aren't just about revealing; they're demonstrative of power and control. The Lamb's ability to open the seals assures disciples that the future is in His hands. All in all, there's quite a bit in this little section, and yet it's just a sampling of what is to come.

PART FOUR

The Sirens of Heaven

In this section, we'll see seven angels sound seven trumpets. As we read about the judgments connected with them, they'll make us think of the plagues that came upon Egypt. Keep in mind the figurative nature of these judgments, and how they are designed to bring about repentance rather than final wrath. When this doesn't happen (9:21), preparations ensue for the ultimate judgment upon Rome.

An angel and an altar (8:2-5)
The sounding of the trumpets (8:6-11:19)

APPEARANCE, REALITY, & PRAYER

"The smoke of the incense, with the prayers of the saints, rose before God from the hand of the angel" (8:4).

Disciples know the importance of prayer. They understand that it changes things and, more importantly, changes them. But they also know there are occasions when it looks as if their prayers have gone unheard by God, and to that degree, prayer seems to be an exercise in futility. "I can't see that my prayers are making any difference, so why bother?" They don't wish to think this way, but they feel compelled to do so by what appears to be overwhelming evidence. With that in mind, there's something quite encouraging in the picture John relates in 8:1-5.

After the seventh seal is opened, there is silence in heaven for half an hour. We don't normally think of heaven as being a quiet place, do we? Jesus talks about angels rejoicing (Luke 15:7, 10). We think of scenes like the ones earlier (Revelation 4-5; 7:9ff) and suggested in texts like Psalm 148:2, "Praise him, all his angels; praise him, all his hosts!" This being the case, the silence stands out and piques our interest as to what is to come.

This quiet is also the calm before the storm. After this pause, John sees the seven angels with seven trumpets, but it's not quite their time yet either (we'll return to them in the next section), so our attention is directed to another angel who is standing before an altar.

He's given "much" incense to offer along with the prayers of "all" God's people. We have this incense/prayer association in Psalm 141:2. We're assured by John in v. 4 that all of this goes up before God. This brings to mind the fifth seal where the martyrs under the altar were crying out to God for their lives to be avenged (6:9-11). We have the same kind of thing going on here; we're being shown that God is aware of all the petitions that have gone up before Him. This would specifically refer to those prayers of the saints calling for justice.

What happens next with the fire from the altar being cast upon the earth is a direct response to those petitions. In many ways, it is a repetition of what we saw earlier in the sixth seal when the "world" of the ungodly was destroyed (6:12-17). The thunder, lightning, and earthquake that follow reinforce the judgmental nature of the casting of fire.

To a member of one of the churches that John is addressing, this scene impresses upon them the vital truth that God is fully aware of all that is going on; He hasn't failed in hearing even the smallest voice that called out to Him. And being omniscient, He knows their situation even better than they do. Just because justice is being delayed so another opportunity for repentance can be extended, doesn't mean it is being denied. The disciples are being powerfully reminded that appearance and reality are not the same thing.

It's a message we still need to hear today.

QUESTIONS

1. Do appearances ever affect our prayers? How?
2. Why do you think incense and prayer are closely related? What does this say about prayer?
3. Take a look at Proverbs 3:5-6 and 2 Corinthians 5:7. How can the principle in these verses help us in dealing with appearances?

JUSTICE, JUDGMENT, & GOOD NEWS

***"Now the seven angels who had the seven trumpets prepared to blow them"* (8:6).**

As the seventh seal is opened, it reveals seven trumpets (just as the seventh trumpet will in turn reveal seven bowls). It's much like a nesting doll: the seals open up to trumpets, which then open up to bowls. We saw six seals opened in Revelation 6 (with multiple scenes involved with the sixth seal in Revelation 7). In the same way, six of the seven trumpets will sound in Revelation 8-9 (with multiple scenes involved with the sixth trumpet in Revelation 10-11). See the pattern? At first glance, Revelation might seem like a chaotic hodgepodge of a book, but it isn't.

The seals, trumpets, and bowls (all seven in number) are symbols that serve to develop the theme of judgment. Just as we saw that Revelation has much to say about worship, it also has multiple sections dealing with judgment upon Rome. These sections show a progression in God's judgment. The seals are about the initial revealing of that judgment, while the trumpets are about calling the unrighteous to repentance. As we'll see later, the bowls represent the pouring out of final judgment upon Rome.

Trumpets were used by Israel for summoning the people, breaking camp, or going into battle (Numbers 10). A trumpet calls the people to the foot of Mt. Sinai to "meet with God" (Exodus 19:16-17 NIV). In all of this, we see that when the trumpet sounded, people were to pay attention so they could respond accordingly. They functioned much like sirens do today when they alert us to look for emergency vehicles or take shelter from threatening weather.

That's the way we're to understand the judgments associated with the sounding of the trumpets. It is not God's wish that any perish but that all come to repentance, and the judgments are designed for getting the attention of the unrighteous. To this point, notice the partial nature of them as a third of the earth is burned up, a third of the sea is turned into blood, a third of the day is without light, etc. (The phrase "a third" is used fifteen times in 8:7-9:18). Because He takes no pleasure in the death of the wicked (Ezekiel 18:23), God imposes less than the full measure of judgment in hope of reformation. It is the same thing judges do when they put someone on probation and/or sentence them to community service. They are hoping to effect a change in behavior so that the maximum sentence won't have to be imposed.

Another thing that stands out is that these judgments bear more than a passing resemblance to the plagues that came upon Egypt. There is hail, water turning into blood, darkness, undrinkable water, aquatic life dying, locusts, etc. But whereas these things literally happened to the Egyptians, I don't think they should be understood that way here (22:18, see the explanation on pp. 84ff). They are symbols of what God will bring upon the unrighteous in an effort to bring them to repentance. We should view them as representative of God's judgment and leave the specific details of their historical outworking to Him.[1]

I think it's accurate to say that, for the most part, both believers and unbelievers are uncomfortable with the judgment of God. Some disciples feel as if they have to apologize for it (as if it reflected an alpha version of God), while unbelievers want no part of it for obvious reasons. Yet justice and judgment are two sides of the same coin. If you believe in

1. And even though the judgment connected with the fifth trumpet will be developed more fully in the next piece, it will still be without historical specifics.

one, you have to believe in the other. It would be great if there were no need for police, courts, or prisons—but since there is a need, it would be unthinkable not to have them! In the same way, judgment is a spiritual reality. It is not the most pleasant subject to think or talk about, but it's part of what makes the good news of Jesus so good.

QUESTIONS

1. How is the theme of judgment against Rome developed in Revelation? Why does it happen this way?
2. How are the judgments like the plagues? How are they unlike them?
3. How are judgment and justice related?

BREAKING BAD

"And the fifth angel blew his trumpet, and I saw a star fallen from heaven to earth, and he was given the key to the shaft of the bottomless pit. He opened the shaft of the bottomless pit, and from the shaft rose smoke like the smoke of a great furnace, and the sun and the air were darkened with the smoke from the shaft. Then from the smoke came locusts on the earth, and they were given power like the power of scorpions of the earth" (9:1-3).

Millions tuned in each week to watch Walter White's descent into the abyss during the five seasons of AMC's *Breaking Bad*. In the show's initial season, White learns he has advanced lung cancer and will probably die soon. He is married, has a teenage son with a disability, and a second child on the way. He is a high school chemistry teacher. He has nowhere near the financial resources needed to pay for expensive medical treatments or provide for his family in the event of his death. In desperation, he turns to manufacturing methamphetamine. Soon, he and a former student, Jesse, have a highly lucrative business.

But that's just the beginning of White's breaking bad as he allows himself to be increasingly sucked into the vortex of evil. His participation in the meth business means living a double life, and his family is repeatedly hurt as a result of his choices and deceitfulness (he misses the birth of his daughter because of a drug deal). He becomes increasingly involved in violence, which over time escalates to murder. He leads others into greater evil (he has Jesse kill for him). He is producing increasing amounts of a substance that brings ruin to the lives of its users and their families, and contributes to the breakdown of society. His cancer goes into remission, but it doesn't matter—White has gone from doing evil to being evil.

We see *Breaking Bad* imaged on a societal scale as the fifth trumpet sounds against Rome in Revelation 9, and the judgment associated with it involves a fallen star being given the key to the Abyss (v. 1). The Abyss is where demons, evil spirits, and fallen angels are consigned; in Luke 8:31 and 2 Peter 2:4, a different word is used for the same region. In other words, it's about the worst place you can imagine.

The star opens the Abyss, and out of it comes darkness and swarms of locusts. In v. 11, we learn that their king is the angel of the Abyss whose name is Destroyer. This is the devil (John 8:44). As king over the Abyss, he has the same kind of authority the star has by virtue of the key he possesses. That's why, from another perspective, the star is also a reference to Satan. As a fallen star, he has no light and is darkness. So we have Satan, darkness, and destruction in this judgment.

If we think about what is being depicted here, there is something even more disturbing than the visual horrors. Satan is granted power (i.e., restraints are removed), and the first thing that happens is that he brings darkness upon the world via smoke that obscures the sun. This is more than physical loss of light; it represents spiritual and moral darkness. Out of it come the locusts to inflict their pain on all who have not been sealed (v. 4). What we see in the fifth trumpet is God allowing spiritual darkness to fall upon Rome, and it results in great pain and suffering.

We like to think that sin is our own idea, and we're totally in control of what we do and the consequences that come as the result of our actions. We're entertained by a character like Walter White precisely because, unlike us, he's out of control. But what we're being told here is that there is more to the sin narrative than just the personal, individual dimension. As part of His judgment against it and us, God allows Satan to ramp up the spiritual darkness that results in further disobedience and destruction to people. This judicial blinding is taught in passages like Romans 1:21-32 and 2 Thessalonians 2:10-12. As we think about different segments of our culture plunging farther and farther into darkness and wonder how long it will be until God brings judgment, it's possible we've missed the point. The sobering truth is that He may already be doing that, and the depth and pain of our plunge is part of God's judgment as restraints have been removed.

This is exactly what He is doing in His judgment upon Rome, and history bears witness to the role moral rot played in their downfall. The lesson we must learn is that while evil might present itself as alluring and our servant (e.g. the locusts with their faces like humans, hair like women, and gold crowns), the reality is that it is a raging beast bent on our destruction (e.g. the locusts have tails with scorpion-like stingers that torment people to the point that they long for the release of death but continue to suffer horribly).

Watching Walter White should be more instructive to us than entertaining.

QUESTIONS

1. What does the fifth trumpet involve?
2. Is moral darkness always the result of people choosing it, or can it come as part of the judgment of God?
3. Why is it a dangerous view to think that we are in control of our sin (Hebrews 3:13)?

FAQ

Are their differences between the judgments of the first four trumpets and the other three?

Yes! Just as there was a four/three split in the seven seals, the eagle's message (8:13) suggests that the final three judgments (spoken of as "woes") will be even worse than the first four. Another difference is that, while the first four affected different parts of the earth, the next two affect man. The seventh trumpet is a bit more involved—victory is declared at its sounding (11:15-19) because it is ultimately connected with the seven bowls of wrath (11:19 / 15:5ff, we'll develop this a bit later).

Keep in mind that the trumpets (except the seventh one) are partial judgments designed to bring repentance. McGuiggan is right—as disturbing as the judgments associated with the trumpet are, it's the people's refusal to repent after experiencing these things that is most alarming (9:20-21). In this, they are no different than Pharaoh was and have brought upon themselves a similar fate.

How can Satan be represented by two images in the vision connected with the fifth trumpet (both the star that has fallen and the angel of the Abyss)?

While it's probably not the way we would choose to speak, we must be careful not to limit John or any of the writers of Scripture to communicating truth only in ways that we are familiar or comfortable with. Having two images represent the same thing is not out of character with other visions in Revelation. In Revelation 6, Jesus is represented by a lamb and as the rider on the white horse. In Revelation 11, God's people are represented by the temple, the altar, and it worshippers (vv. 1-2). Then in v. 3ff, we transition to two witnesses (who also represent the church).

Incidentally, it works the other way too. Sometimes, a single image can represent two different things (17:9-10). In all of this, we see there is an elasticity to Revelation that takes some getting used to.

EAT IT—IT'S GOOD FOR YOU

***"So I went to the angel and told him to give me the little scroll. And he said to me, 'Take and eat it; it will make your stomach bitter, but in your mouth it will be sweet as honey.' And I took the little scroll from the hand of the angel and ate it. It was sweet as honey in my mouth, but when I had eaten it my stomach was made bitter"* (10:9-10).**

The messenger is identified by John as "another mighty angel." This takes us back to 5:2, where a mighty angel asked who was worthy to break the seals and open the scroll. Following Bauckham, I think the scroll (now unsealed and open) is being reintroduced. He points out how the scroll has followed the order of 1:1—going from God to Jesus (5:7), then to the angel, and finally to John (10:1, 9).

We've seen the impenitence of the wicked, and their failure to respond to the preliminary and partial judgments of the trumpets. The window on repentance is now closed, and final judgment is about to transpire. Therefore, the angel raises his right hand to God, swearing by Him "that there would be no more delay" (v. 6).

There's something indescribably sad about people being given every opportunity to change, yet continually choosing to turn their backs upon their Father until they reach a point of no return. It's Jesus crying outside Jerusalem. It's heaven weeping for forty days in the time of Noah. It's God looking for enough righteous people to spare Sodom and Gomorrah. We learn from those events as well as from this picture that, while God's patience is more than remarkable, it is not infinite. More to the point, sin is a spiritual black hole that sucks us in and eats away at our desire to do good and follow God. It is where hope can be destroyed.

John is to continue boldly proclaiming his message (note the "again" of v. 11). In a picture reminiscent of Ezekiel 2-3, he is told to take the scroll from the angel's hand and eat it. It is sweet in his mouth because it is the word of God, but bitter in his stomach because proclaiming judgment (even to those who deserve it) is a difficult thing to do (see Ezekiel 3:14-15). By eating it, John is submitting himself to God's mission for him (Ezekiel 2:8).

There's a message here for disciples. If we're to be salt and light, we too must internalize God's message. The fast food approach to Scripture creates faith a mile long and an inch deep, doing little for its practitioners and nothing for the world. If we are to engage the world, we must engage the Word.

And if we are to engage the world, we must not marginalize them into positions, issues, or lifestyles. Instead we must see them as God does—as people deeply loved and made to image Him. We're not to back off truth in any way, shape, or form (that wouldn't be healthy or Christ-like), but we must learn to listen empathically if we are to share effectively. Too many times, believers are content to speak at the level of conclusions to a world that hasn't heard the premises, and the results are predictable—much more heat than light. We must start where people are.

Sadly, not everyone will respond. The rebellious will appreciate neither the message nor the messenger. Rather than overreact to their decisions, disciples must stay the course of kindness, goodness, and self-control. If people are to reject Christ, let it be about Him and not about us.

QUESTIONS

1. What is the angel's message, and what does it mean in the context of Revelation? Why do you think some people refuse to repent?
2. What is the significance of John eating the scroll? What does this say to us?
3. How can we maintain the right attitude when people reject Christ?

A MEASURED REMEMBRANCE

***"In the days of the trumpet call to be sounded by the seventh angel, the mystery of God would be fulfilled, just as he announced to his servants the prophets"* (10:7).**

There are a couple of things about this verse that are important. To begin with, it tells us when this judgment will take place: when the seventh angel sounds his trumpet. As we'll see, the seventh trumpet ultimately leads to the seven bowls being poured out (11:19; 15:5ff). This was the same thing we saw with the opening of the seventh seal revealing the seven angels with their trumpets (8:1, 6). All of this underscores the truth that the previous judgments were partial, and the lack of repentance has now led God to respond to His people's cries for justice.

This verse also informs us as to what is taking place; it is the mystery announced through the prophets. This furnishes us with an important interpretive key to understanding Revelation. "Mystery" refers to some previously hidden or under-developed truth. In Daniel 2, Daniel hears about Nebuchadnezzar's dream from one of his officials, but like the king, has no clue as to its meaning. He and his friends seek God's help in understanding the dream. Their prayer is answered, and the mystery is revealed to them (vv. 15-19). This is representative of the way "mystery" is used in Scripture (see Romans 16:25ff; 1 Corinthians 2:7 NIV; 15:51).

What John is being told with these words is that some previously obscure truth (mystery) is being accomplished and realized in the judgment being enacted upon Rome. This encourages us to view Revelation as the fuller development of Old Testament texts such a Daniel 2, 7. This confirms that the way to understand Revelation isn't by looking forward and playing guessing games about events in the Mid-East, Russia, or some other country. We understand it by looking back to the prophets like Daniel and seeing how Revelation syncs with what they had to say.

Most of us aren't much on looking back. There's something healthy about that. As someone said, "You can't live life backwards. That's why the windshield is bigger than the rear view mirror." We've all heard talk about the good ol' days (as though there was nothing else) and noticed that people preoccupied with such speech are often lost in the present.

Nonetheless, there's value in knowing the past. If we approach it in the right way, it becomes, not an anchor to weigh us down, but a rudder to guide us. What's true for understanding Revelation is true for life; we need such a measured remembrance to fully appreciate the hope that's before us.

QUESTIONS

1. How is the word "mystery" used in Scripture? What is the mystery that is being spoken of here? How does this help us in understanding Revelation?
2. When is looking back a bad thing? When is it a good thing?

FAQ

What did the voices of the seven thunders say, and why wasn't John permitted to write it down?

This is what makes Revelation, Revelation.

Of course, no one knows what was said. Since we're in a judgment text, and it was the voices of thunder speaking, it wouldn't be unreasonable to assume that it was something along the lines of judgment. Bauckham suggests that, in light of what follows (the "no more delay" statement by the angel), the voices of thunder speak of another partial judgment to give the wicked further opportunity to repent. I think the real question that should be asked is, why is this a part of Revelation? John heard something, and he was going to write it down and was told not to—what's the point in telling us that?

Some have suggested that this lets us know that God's judgment is more than what is revealed to John; it reminds us how God is acting in more ways than we know. That makes sense to me and is an important truth to keep in mind in everything. God has revealed to us many marvelous things, but there are "secret things" which belong to Him alone (Deuteronomy 29:29). We would do well to remember His provision and our limitations.

IF THE LORD HAD NOT BEEN ON OUR SIDE...

***"Then I was given a measuring rod like a staff, and I was told, 'Rise and measure the temple of God and the altar and those who worship there, but do not measure the court outside the temple; leave that out, for it is given over to the nations, and they will trample the holy city for forty-two months"* (11:1-2).**

John goes from taking a book and eating it to measuring the temple and its worshippers. Initially, this seems unrelated, but it's not. Remember, we're still dealing with the sixth trumpet and the failure of the ungodly to repent. In response, John has received his commission to disclose the judgment written on the scroll. Now we're being taken to the temple where we'll see two witnesses protected by God while they give their testimony—exactly what John and the churches are being called to do in Revelation.

To the ancients, measuring something was not about finding out its size, but was a metaphor for marking it off and separating it from everything else. Think about how lines are marked on a football field or a baseball diamond to set it off from the area around it, and you have the idea. John is to measure the temple and the worshippers, but the exterior courtyard is to be left alone.

Why? It has been "given" to the Gentiles (v. 2 NIV). If you've made it this far, you know I think the Gentiles are Rome, and the truth that is being pictured here is that nothing will happen that will take God by surprise. Rome's oppression of the church (represented by the temple, worshippers, and courtyard) will occur only because God permits it. And while it will be significant (the courtyard/holy city is "trampled on"), it's also partial. What's at its heart (the temple and its worshippers) will be sustained. There are boundaries or limits on what God will allow. We're being reminded of the same truth that Jesus told Pilate—Rome has no power other than what has been given to it, and there are limits on that!

It seems that the last part of this truth is especially underrated. The Scripture speaks in other places of God setting limits (Job 1:12; 2:6; Matthew 24:22). Who hasn't looked at the rubble left by a tornado and wondered how anyone survived? Or maybe we've marveled that someone was able to walk away from a car accident where the vehicles were totaled? It's right to focus on the losses that do occur at such times (how could we not?), but somewhere down the line it's also healthy to think about what didn't happen and give thanks for that. Haven't we all experienced situations that should have turned out much worse than they did?

This is one of those truths that we acknowledge in the here and now and will understand fully later. In Psalm 124, David considers what would have happened "if the Lord had not been on our side" (vv. 1-2 NIV). After acknowledging what would have occurred (vv. 3-5), he praises God (v. 6) and concludes with, "Our help is in the name of the LORD, who made heaven and earth" (v. 8). That's the truth John is reminding his readers of and that we need to hold in our hearts.

QUESTIONS

1. What truth did measuring something convey in John's time? What does it mean that the temple, altar, and its worshippers are measured?
2. Do you think God still "marks things off" today? Why or why not?

WORSHIP & WITNESS

"And I will grant authority to my two witnesses, and they will prophesy for 1,260 days, clothed in sackcloth" (11:3).

Two witnesses clothed in sackcloth (due to mourning their situation) are introduced. They will prophesy for 1,260 days. As McGuiggan notes, the witnesses have characteristics of:

- Moses and Aaron (they can turn water into blood and strike the earth with plagues)
- Elijah and Elisha (calling down fire, 1 Kings 18; 2 Kings 1)
- Joshua and Zerubbabel (two olive trees and lampstands, Zechariah 3-4)

All of these duos stood for God during turbulent times—exactly what the seven churches are being called to do. Therefore, the witnesses represent the people of God just as the temple (and all that goes with it) does. And just as the outer court of the temple was trampled upon by Rome, so the prophets will be slain by the beast from the Abyss, but not before they have finished their testimony (v. 7). And after their bodies have been displayed for their enemies to rejoice over for 3½ days, God will resurrect them and bring judgment in the form of a severe earthquake.

So this picture expands upon the temple image by adding a couple of elements: a resurrection and a judgment.

While these images convey the same essential message (that God will deliver His people through, not from, difficult times), they approach it from different perspectives. The temple image speaks to worship, while the duo in sackcloth has to do with witness. Both aspects of discipleship are under attack in the Roman culture. Worship was threatened by all of the social/economic/political inducements to offer homage to the various gods, from the imperial cult to pagan deities (Artemis, Zeus, etc.). Witness—faithfully proclaiming the testimony of Jesus—would be difficult under such circumstances. Keeping silent would be the prudent course of action in such conditions. Witness flows from worship, and the church kept right on with both. They didn't play it safe, and neither can we.

The Book of Eli covers the familiar ground of post-apocalyptic movies: bleak new world, humanity's descent into savagery, and the struggle for scarce resources (with goodness being the rarest). Where it is different is that it has a decidedly spiritual/Christian element to it. And with Hollywood, you're never quite sure where that is going to lead.

As it turns out, it's neither good nor bad; it's somewhere in between. On the one hand, the movie's central character, Eli, is committed to God, goodness, and his mission. On the other hand, he's an absolute killing machine, which seems to be connected with his calling. Apparently, his practice of faith recognizes no gradation of punishment or alternate means of dealing with evil—everyone opposed just gets killed.

The best parts of the movie for me were the scenes where the story focused on the book in Eli's possession (i.e., the Bible). Carnegie, the wicked man who wants the book, explains to Eli why he has to have it.

> *I grew up with it. I know its power. And if you read it, then so do you. That's why they burned them all after the war. Just staying alive is an act of faith. Building this town is an even bigger act of faith. But they don't understand that. None of*

> *them. And I don't have the right words to help them, but the book does. Now, I admit that I've had to do things, many, many things that I hate to build this—I confess that. But if we have that book, I wouldn't have to. Now imagine, imagine how different, how righteous this little world could be ... if we had the right words for our faith. The people would truly understand why they're here ... and they wouldn't need any of the uglier motivations. It's not right to keep that book hidden away. It's meant to be shared with others. It's meant to be spread. Isn't that what you want?*

Interesting, don't you think? And there's much truth in those words, but it's all a ruse. Carnegie says the right things, but his heart (and his head) aren't in it. Once away from Eli, he tells his men, "It's a weapon—a weapon aimed right at the hearts and minds of the weak and desperate. It will give us control of them."

Eli is not without fault (though, to his credit, he recognizes it). In a pivotal scene, he finally reveals to Carnegie where the book is hidden, but only when the life of his friend, Solara, is threatened. She tells him, "I didn't think anything could make you give up that book. I thought it was too important."

Eli tells her, "All the years I've been carrying it and reading it every day ... I got so caught up in keeping it safe, I forgot to live by what I learned from it."

There you have it. Carnegie can say the right words, but he doesn't believe them. Eli believes them, but fails to translate them into life because he is concerned about "keeping it safe." Although there are always those who, like Carnegie, will use the Scripture for their own twisted purposes, I think most of us share in Eli's struggle—we're also caught up in "keeping it safe," rather than heeding the radical call of Scripture.

Keeping it safe is not what we're called to do. We're called to find life through losing it. We're called to pray for His kingdom to come and His will to be done. Loving people unconditionally is not always safe. Serving people isn't always easy. These things brought a cross to Jesus, and we're called to follow in His steps (1 Peter 2:20-21).

A faith that costs nothing carries the same return. May our worship and witness bring glory to Him.

QUESTIONS

1. The temple imagery and the two clothed in sackcloth speak to what two aspects of the disciple's life? How were these under attack in Revelation?
2. What are some ways that believers get caught up in "keeping it safe"? How can we overcome this?

SUBMARINES & KINGDOMS

***"The kingdom of the world has become the kingdom of our Lord and of his Christ, and he shall reign forever and ever"* (11:15).**

We're told in 11:14 that the second woe is passed, and that the third is about to come. Since the three woes are connected with the last three trumpets (8:13), we know the seventh trumpet is about to sound. Furthermore, we were told by the mighty angel that with the sounding of the seventh trumpet "there would be no more delay" (10:6). Therefore, when we hear loud voices in heaven that tell us, "The kingdom of the world has become the kingdom of our Lord and of His Christ" (v. 15), we shouldn't be surprised (even though we're only halfway through the book). Just as the opening of the seventh seal brought with it the seven trumpets, the sounding of the seventh trumpet brings into play the pouring out of the seven bowls of final judgment upon Rome.

With this judgment, the kingdom of the world (Rome) has been vanquished by the kingdom of the Lord. The 24 elders say to God, "You have taken your great power and begun to reign" (v. 17). This is hardly suggesting that the reign of God didn't begin until Rome was judged—you'd have to ignore texts like 1 Chronicles 29:11ff; Isaiah 37:16; the entire book of Daniel, etc. to reach this conclusion. God has always ruled. Nor is it saying that God would begin ruling through Jesus at this time, because we've already been told He rules in 1:5; 2:26-27; 3:21, etc. What, then, is being said?

It's the same kind of truth that's stated in Luke 21:31 where Jesus speaks of the kingdom of God being near. In the context, He's talking about the destruction of Jerusalem in A.D. 70 (vv. 20, 32). This was God's judgment on the unbelieving Jewish nation (Luke 19:41ff; Matthew 23:37-39). The kingdom was near in the sense that the judgment would be a manifestation/demonstration of God's already existing rule. The same thing is being said here by the 24 elders. God is already ruling through Jesus Christ. With Rome's judgment, that reign will be manifested in a powerful, visible way.

Think of a submarine and how it does the majority of its work beneath the water—present and active, but invisible. Every so often, it rises up from the deep, and we see more clearly a reality that we were already aware of through sonar and other technology. The kingdom of God is like that. It is present, active, and to a large degree, invisible. But with the judgments upon Jerusalem and Rome, it rises above the waterline, and we see a visible manifestation of what we were already aware of through faith.

This brings us back to appearance versus reality. To these seven struggling churches, Rome's towering presence must have seemed omnipotent at times, but it wasn't. From the Roman point of view, these little communities were at most a source of irritation and at least, next to nothing. Their little kingdom hardly registered a blip on Rome's radar. Revelation provides us with a stark reminder that these appearances are just that, and history bears out the reality of the true eternal kingdom.

QUESTIONS

1. How is the kingdom of God like a submarine?
2. What does this remind us about appearance and reality?

FAQ

How should we understand the 42 months during which the Gentiles trample on the holy city? Is it related to the 1,260 days that the two witnesses prophesy?

If you've made it this far in the book, you know that Revelation is full of numbers. There are two approaches we can take when we come across them. We can understand them as simply representing numerical values (their normal meaning to us), or we can see them as symbolizing something else.

For example, the seven churches belong in the first category since we're given their locations, specific details about their spiritual health, and the corrective measures that need to be taken. The 144,000 we've come across a few times would belong in the second category since it isn't meant to be taken as a literal number, but rather is a symbol of completeness (i.e., all of God's people).

The 42 months, 1,260 days, and even the 3½ days that the bodies of the two witnesses lay unburied in the city all belong to the second category—they are symbols. In fact, it doesn't seem that they have anything to do with an amount of time, but rather represent a state of being (McGuiggan). The 42 months and 1,260 days are the same thing, just expressed in different units of measure. But the best way to think of them is to use another measure, for they're equal to 3½ years. And what is 3½? It's a broken seven. It's not perfection, completion, wholeness, etc. It's the opposite. Therefore, these are symbols of the incompleteness of Rome's power. It's there, it's real, and it may win the moment, but it will not win the day. I think that's what we're supposed to see when these numbers are brought before us. They have nothing to do with time and everything to do with the limitations of Rome's oppression of the saints.

We see this same thing in regard to the bodies of the two witnesses that lay unburied in the city for 3½ days before they are resurrected. They can be killed, but they can't be contained. Rome's triumph over them is as partial as its triumph over Jesus.

Isn't the great city where the Lord was crucified (v. 8) referring to Jerusalem?

"Great city" is found eight times in Revelation, and we're told that it:

- rules over the kings of the earth (17:18)
- sits on seven hills (17:18, 9)
- is where all who had ships became rich through her wealth (18:19)

All of this should be enough to help us see that the "great city" is Rome, rather than Jerusalem. Furthermore, notice that it is associated with the beast that comes out of the Abyss (vv. 7-8), which we'll see is also a symbol of Rome in Revelation 13.

Why does John speak the way he does? I can think of a few possibilities. One is that this might be emphasizing Rome's part in the crucifixion, since a Roman official (Pilate) made the decision that Jesus would die, and Roman soldiers carried it out. Remembering that we're in a book admittedly given toward figurative speech, this shouldn't be quickly dismissed. It may not be the way we would choose to communicate such a truth, but then how many of us speak the way John does in Revelation?

Another approach is that Rome is symbolized by Sodom and Egypt, and Jesus was "crucified" in these places by their immorality and oppression. The Hebrews writer speaks of people who had been disciples crucifying Jesus again though their rejection of Him (6:4ff).

The view that currently resonates with me the most is that the great city is immoral (like Sodom), oppressive (like Egypt), and is crucifying Jesus (like Jerusalem). By bringing death to the disciples, Rome is crucifying Jesus (Acts 9:1-6).

Who is the beast that comes up from the Abyss and kills the two witnesses (v. 7)?

You wouldn't be too surprised if I said it was Rome, would you? We'll see the beast in great detail in Revelation 13, 17. For now, it's worth noting that there are three things introduced in Revelation 11 that we'll see significantly more of: the beast, the holy city, and the broken seven.

What have we seen?

In this second section of judgment, we've been reminded by an angel at an altar that justice delayed is not justice denied. We've seen six trumpets sound and partial judgment come upon the wicked in an attempt to bring them to repentance. This doesn't happen, so John eats the scroll of judgment while the church is braced by God to continue to bear witness. The seventh trumpet sounds, and it's the beginning of the end for Domitian and Rome.

PART FIVE

The Beginning of the End

In a sense, the judgment aspect of the book is completed with the sounding of the seventh trumpet as it leads to the seven bowls of wrath being poured out. This is why the eleventh chapter closes with the proclamation of victory (11:15). What remains is to show the outworking of this judgment from different vantage points as we're told that "the time has come" for rewarding and destroying (11:18 NIV). That's what we'll see in this section as new images continue to be imported into the story.

The woman, dragon, and the child (12:1-17)
The two beasts (13:1-18)
144,000, 3 angels, and 2 harvests (14:1-20)

CRUSHED OR CONQUERING?

"And a great sign appeared in heaven: a woman clothed with the sun, with the moon under her feet, and on her head a crown of twelve stars. She was pregnant and was crying out in birth pains and the agony of giving birth. And another sign appeared in heaven: behold, a great red dragon, with seven heads and ten horns, and on his heads seven diadems" (12:1-3).

This section begins with more incredible imagery spread across three scenes. It continues the theme of conflict and conquering, as well as develops a truth that has only been touched upon up to this point—the satanic presence behind the Empire. There are three figures in these scenes: a woman, a dragon, and the child born to the woman.

The woman is introduced in association with light. She is clothed with the sun, has the moon under her feet, and twelve stars on her head. Light is a common figure for the people of God (Matthew 5:14ff; Philippians 2:14ff), and the number of the stars on her head reinforces this identity as it aligns her with the twelve tribes of Israel and the apostles of Jesus.

In a gruesome aspect of the picture, the dragon waits for the woman to give birth so he can devour her baby. From this and other information we're given, it's not hard to see that the dragon represents Satan. He has seven heads and ten horns. We'll see in Revelation 13 that the beast that rises up out of the sea (Rome) is described in the same manner. Satan is being portrayed in this way so that when we see the beast, we'll know exactly who it is allied with.

Finally, there's the child who is born of the woman "who is to rule all the nations" (v. 5). The dragon tries to seize him, but is unsuccessful as the son is "caught up to God and to His throne" (v. 5). This son clearly represents Jesus. So we have in this picture the people of God, Satan, Jesus, conflict, and deliverance.

After the child is snatched up to God, the woman flees into the desert to "a place prepared by God, in which she is to be nourished for 1,260 days" (v. 6). Notice we're back to the 3½ years that were introduced in the previous chapter. Though the woman is in the desert (indicating hardship), she's in a place God has prepared for her so that she might be taken care of.

The message is the same one that we've been hearing throughout the book—the people of God are in for a rough time, but God will see them through it. Satan was unable to get God's Son, and he won't fare any better with His family.

I don't know that we often think of the vulnerability of Jesus as is pictured here, but we should. I suspect that more often than not, we see Him calming the sea, raising the dead, and generally gliding through life by virtue of His miraculous abilities. If that's the case, then there's another layer of His life that we need to see. As a baby and later a young boy, Jesus needed the protection God provided Him through His parents and others. Although this changed when He became an adult, His vulnerability didn't cease. Being human meant that He was exposed to Satan through temptation, persecution, betrayal, and His death on the cross. Any of these things had the potential to destroy Him if He didn't trust in His Father's purposes. But instead of being crushed, He conquered.

John wants us to see that God intends for His story to be our story.

QUESTIONS

1. Who is the pregnant woman clothed in light? Who is her son?
2. What is the conflict in the picture? How is it resolved? What message does this have for John's readers? For us?

THIS IS HOW WE OVERCOME

"They have conquered him by the blood of the Lamb" (12:11).

John's not finished by any means—he has more to say about the dragon. In the second part of his vision, he sees a war break out in heaven with the dragon and his angels fighting against Michael and his angels. This is a continuation of what we were introduced to in vv. 1-6, as the dragon is now continuing its pursuit of Jesus into heaven. Once again the dragon is unsuccessful ("he was not strong enough," v. 8 NIV), and he and his angels are thrown to earth (v. 9). The overarching truth we're to see is that the dragon is defeated twice (on earth and in heaven) in his efforts to destroy Jesus.

This is followed by a voice from heaven proclaiming victory ("Now have come the salvation and the power and the kingdom of our God, and the authority of His Messiah," v. 10 NIV). Of course, these things have existed previously, but they're now being manifested (again) through Satan's defeat. Verse 11 extends this victory to the followers of Jesus, who triumphed because of their testimony, their devotion to God above even their own lives, and the initial reason John gives—"the blood of the Lamb."

Our hope is not in ourselves! No one would dare to think such a thing in the face of adversity, when the crush of circumstances has brought us to our knees. We are all too well aware of our vulnerability at the hospital, the unemployment line, or the cemetery. But many find it difficult to acknowledge God to the same degree in times of prosperity.

It's remarkably easy to lapse into an "I've got this covered Lord," mindset. Nebuchadnezzar was a Babylonian king used by God to discipline the Jewish nation. Despite being informed by Daniel that his reign was the result of God's will rather than his own (Daniel 2:37-38), and that he would lose his rule by failing to acknowledge this truth (4:24-27), Nebuchadnezzar nonetheless descends into such a state (4:28-30). A period of time living among the wild animals and munching grass reminded him who the real power was.

This is a problem that affects far more than just Babylonian kings!

QUESTIONS

1. How does the dragon continue to pursue Jesus? What message should we get from his defeat?
2. What are the reasons John gives for disciples being victorious over Satan?
3. Why do you think it's so easy for us to lapse into an "I've got this covered, Lord" mentality?

WAITING FOR DEATH

***"They have conquered him ... for they loved not their lives even unto death"* (12:11).**

Movies by the Coen brothers tend to leave me hot or cold, but never lukewarm. *No Country for Old Men* is no exception. It's a dark movie (maybe their darkest), but it has something to say, especially in the character of Sheriff Ed Tom Bell.

The story (adapted from the novel by Cormac McCarthy) is a simple one that incorporates some of the more sinister aspects of fallen man: the exploitation, suffering, and bondage brought about by the drug trade, the disregard and depersonalizing of life via contract killing, and the pervasive greed that fuels it all. Give the Coens credit for showing the putrid, destructive nature of it all.

It's 1980, and Llewelyn Moss is a Vietnam veteran who stumbles across a drug deal gone bad in the open country of west Texas where there is nothing but dead bodies and $2 million in cash. He takes the bag containing the money, unaware there is a transmitter hidden inside. Soon, both sides are in pursuit of him—a group of faceless Mexicans representing one side, and a hit man named Anton Chigurh working for the other side. Chigurh is deranged, diabolical, and there is a relentlessness to his pursuit of Moss that is unnerving. In pursuit of both Chigurh and Moss is Sheriff Bell.

Ed Tom Bell is older than either of the two men he is after. In fact, he is contemplating retirement. But it's not age that's pushing this decision; it's weariness. He not only feels he's fighting a losing battle against evil, but he's in one that he no longer understands. He says:

> *I don't know what to make of that. I sure don't. The crime you see now, it's even hard to take its measure. It's not that I'm afraid of it. I always knew you had to be willing to die even to do this job. But I don't want to push my chips forward and go out and meet something I don't understand. Man would have to put his soul at hazard. He'd have to say, "Okay, I'll be a part of this world."*

As a result, he half-heartedly pursues them and is always a step behind. The climax of the movie occurs when Bell walks into a motel room where Chigurh is hiding behind the door. He makes no attempt to check behind the door, exposing his back to Chigurh, while he goes to check out the bathroom and sees that the window there is locked from the inside. Chigurh makes his escape unnoticed, and Bell wrongly concludes that Chigurh left before he arrived. He reholsters his gun, sits on the bed and lets out a sigh of relief. He notices that the air conditioning return vent has been opened and understands that not only has the killer eluded him, but he also made off with the money that was hidden there. He has learned what we already know from his failure to detect Chigurh in the room and the plodding way he has handled the case; it is no country for old men, or at least, not old men like him. Shortly after this, Bell retires, and the movie ends with him having nothing to do but wait for death.

If you are following Jesus, you are in a war. This is a reality religious consumers choose not to embrace, but something disciples must understand. Wars are not pretty, neat, or packaged. They are chaotic, bloody, and exhausting in a way that nothing else is. They are about surviving, rescuing others, and defeating opposing forces.

It's very possible that there will come a time when you will feel like Ed Tom Bell. You will feel overwhelmed, discouraged, and possibly even defeated. Like Sheriff Bell, you won't feel like surrendering—you just don't want to fight anymore. Elijah experienced all of this in 1 Kings 19:1-4. Church membership rolls contain the names of countless people who fit this description. Once their faith was alive, vital, and pushing them and others forward in the kingdom of God. Then they were wounded by the enemy, worn down by the battle, or maybe even shot by friendly fire. Whatever the cause, they retreated and haven't been back to the battle since. Like Ed Tom Bell, they are just waiting for death.

I'm guessing this is how the disciples felt after Jesus' death. "If the world has become so evil that they killed the Teacher and Healer, what's the point? What difference can we make?"

The answer is, much more than they could imagine!

The resurrection changed everything for them and us. Weariness and despondency (and all other opponents), were defeated by Jesus Christ one Sunday morning outside Jerusalem. When everything was said and done, they were in the grave, and He had risen.

In this life, we face very real foes that seek our destruction. God would not allow that to happen to His Son, and won't allow it to happen to His followers. That said, we need to keep in close contact with our Leader. And it's never a good move to separate ourselves from the rest of the troops. Strength is in numbers, because the enemy likes to isolate and intimidate. Ed Tom Bell could tell us all about that.

We have something to do besides wait for death! Like the first-century faithful, we can refuse to shrink from death by giving our lives fully to the King and His cause.

QUESTIONS

1. Do you think Christians are generally aware that they are in a war? Why or why not?
2. What passages of Scripture can you think of that use a war metaphor for some aspect of following Jesus?
3. Have you ever felt like Elijah did in 1 Kings 19? How was he helped? What does this say to us?

TRIUMPHANT SUFFERING

"They have conquered him ... for they loved not their lives even unto death" **(12:11).**

Triumphant suffering is one of the paradoxes of the kingdom that tends to be harder to grasp than some of the other ones (i.e., the first shall be last, it is more blessed to give than receive, etc). I suppose this has to do with at least a couple of things.

One would be that our bodies are obviously wired in such a way that we instinctively move away from pain and toward comfort (and in the big picture, this is a very good thing). Additionally, we live in a culture that caters to the idea of a pain-free existence as the only acceptable way of living. Commercials assure us that if we have the slightest ache or pain, we can consult our physician about the latest, greatest medication, and if we don't grow a second head or a third arm, it could help us to be pain-free! (This has absolutely nothing to say to those dealing with severe pain and suffering.)

And while what I've said has to do specifically with physical suffering rather than some other kind (psychological, emotional, spiritual, etc.), it seems that our mindset is essentially the same for all. There's little or no place for suffering in our biography or theology. We've bought into the idea that life is meant to be an unending stream of pleasantries.

Qualify that in any way you feel the need to, but what remains is our resistance to the reality that suffering is part of the disciple's call (Philippians 1:29-30; 1 Peter 2:20-21, etc.). Consequently, those who do suffer are relegated to viewing their situation as a sub-status existence, and the total focus becomes changing their circumstances (see Paul's struggle with this in 2 Corinthians 12:7ff). Indeed, I've heard many people lament that in such a situation, they were "of no use" to God. They didn't get such an idea from Scripture, and certainly not from Revelation!

As many have pointed out, the dominant symbol for Christ in the book is not a lion (used one time), but a lamb (used over twenty times). But more than that, it is a lamb "looking as if it had been slain" because it had been (5:6 NIV). To put an even finer point on it, it was through such suffering that He overcame, and we are assured in 12:11 that those disciples who overcame did so because "they did not love their lives so much as to shrink from death" (NIV).

Where does this leave us? Hopefully, we will have, not only the faith to believe that our Father is powerful enough to bring us out of any suffering that's not His will, but also to trust that He can bring us through any suffering that is in line with His holy purposes. Where I come from, it takes more faith to believe the second than the first.

This is a hard truth, but I've seen people live it. More than that, I've seen them stand courageously and inspire others. My friend Cecil had throat cancer that necessitated radical surgery. This was followed by 33 radiation treatments, the medical equivalent of a scorched earth policy. When it was all over, he had a tube in his stomach and a fire in his throat that wouldn't go away. But the real pain came when he lost his wife of 53 years, the woman who had nursed him through his illness. Through it all, he remained brave and kept his eyes on the Lord. As of this writing, Cecil is doing well and continuing to point us in heaven's direction.

We can help people like Cecil (and ourselves) by accepting that, just as God had a purpose for the cross of Jesus, He will use whatever we encounter, even though we might have no clue how He will do that.

We also need to proclaim loudly that suffering (which is isolating enough as it is) cannot make us sub-status if it links us with our Lord! Finally, we must stop praying exclusively that our loved ones be healed; we must hold them up to the Father for courage, for comfort, and for strength for whatever His will might be (Acts 4:27-31). If these things are done, the sufferer can experience more call and calm and less calamity.

QUESTIONS

1. "Suffering is part of the disciple's call." What passages can you think of that support this? Why do you think this truth isn't emphasized much?
2. Can you think of someone who has handled their suffering courageously? What effect did this have on others?
3. What do Philippians 1:29-30 and 1 Peter 2:20-21 teach us about suffering?

WHEN HOPE & HISTORY COME TOGETHER

***"And when the dragon saw that he had been thrown down to the earth, he pursued the woman who had given birth to the male child. But the woman was given the two wings of the great eagle so that she might fly from the serpent into the wilderness, to the place where she is to be nourished for a time, and times, and half a time"* (12:13-14).**

In the first two parts of John's vision in Revelation 12, we've seen Satan defeated on earth and in heaven. In v. 12, we are warned that he is "filled with fury" (NIV), and the final scene of John's vision (vv. 13-17) conveys how this works out.

The dragon pursues the woman (the people of God). The woman is given the "wings of a great eagle" (Exodus 19:4) so that she might escape to the place prepared for her in the wilderness. "Wilderness" conveys the concept of hardship, while "prepared" reminds us that God is sustaining His people through it all. We're told she would be out of the serpent's reach for "time, times, and half a time" (v. 14). This is yet another way of saying 3½, and we've seen it used repeatedly (11:2, 3, 9) to refer to Rome's oppression of the church. With it, we're being reminded of the limited nature of the enemy's power.

In response to the woman's flight, the dragon spews water "like a river" in an effort to destroy her (v. 15). But just as in the exodus of Israel from Egypt, a little water doesn't get in the way of God delivering His people. The earth aids the woman by swallowing the water. The dragon is once again defeated and goes off to make war against other believers (v. 17), possibly a reference to disciples outside the seven churches to which John is writing.

With this, we have seen the dragon go down to defeat three times. The message is clear: the forces of evil cannot and will not be victorious! Rome will oppress, but will not win. This was hope for the disciples of John's day, and it's history for ours.

It's never a bad thing when hope and history come together. It's the bride walking down the aisle toward her groom. It's a young person walking across the stage with a diploma in his or her hands. It's someone rising up out of the water with new life through Jesus. One of the great values of Revelation for us today is that it shows hope and history coming together.

We need all we can get of that.

QUESTIONS

1. How do hope and history come together in the three-part story of Revelation 12?
2. How does knowing the history of God's people provide us with hope (Romans 15:4)?

FAQ

What does the "third of the stars" (v. 4) that the dragon swats out of the sky with his tail have reference to?

There are almost as many different views on this as there are stars in the sky! Some think it refers to angels, others suggest political power, and there are those who think it refers to part of the Jewish world. Of course, any determination of the meaning will depend on how you've understood Revelation up to this point. For that reason, it makes sense to me to see stars that have been struck down as some of God's people. We have a precedent for such an understanding in Daniel 8:10, 24, where Daniel uses stars to represent Jewish believers put to death by the Seleucid king, Antiochus IV Epiphanies.

This picture points us to the sobering realities that the dragon (Satan) is powerful, deadly, and not to be trifled with. In doing these things, it also implicitly celebrates the power of the One who has defeated him and reminds us of our constant need for a savior.

Are vv. 7-9 an allusion to Satan's fall from heaven?

Certain elements in these scenes appear to be inspired by actual events. The dragon attempting to devour the new born child reminds us of King Herod seeking to have Jesus killed after His birth. The woman fleeing into the desert could be based on Israel's flight or Elijah's time there. Although parts of these scenes might spring from some historical basis, the overall scene itself is not history, is not meant to be understood that way, and it doesn't have to be to communicate spiritual truth.

It is like the story of the Good Samaritan or the Prodigal Son. These stories contain historical truths (there were priests and Levites, inheritance laws, etc.), but that doesn't mean we're to take these parables as historical. In the same sense, this is a vision intended to communicate the truth that the dragon (Satan) is a loser. He fails to snatch the baby, is repulsed from heaven, and is unable to capture the woman.

FOLLOW THE HORN, PART 1

***"I considered the horns, and behold, there came up among them another horn, a little one, before which three of the first horns were plucked up by the roots. And behold, in this horn were eyes like the eyes of a man, and a mouth speaking great things"* (Daniel 7:8).**

If we could return to *The Wizard of Oz* for a moment, you'll remember Glinda telling Dorothy that the wizard is the only one who can get her back to Kansas. He resides in the Emerald City, and the way to get there is to "follow the Yellow Brick Road." The munchkins sing their agreement, and off goes Dorothy skipping down the road with her dog, Toto, following along. In the same way, if we'll follow the eleventh horn of Daniel 7, it won't lead us to the Emerald City or the wizard, but it will allow us to set the book of Revelation in its historical context. And when you think about all of the controversy and confusion that seems to swirl continually around Revelation, anchoring it in such a manner is critical, as it will keep us from drifting all over the place in our efforts to understand it.

In Daniel 2, Nebuchadnezzar has the disturbing dream of the four-part statue that Daniel tells him are four kingdoms starting with his (Babylon). The next two are Medo-Persia and Macedonia (Greece). The fourth kingdom will be strong and conquer all the others; each kingdom conquers and absorbs the preceding one so that the fourth kingdom is said to "crush and break all the others" (v. 40 NIV). This is Rome.

During the days of those kings (plural possibly because it refers to the different rulers of Rome but more likely because it refers to the rulers of the preceding kingdoms who lived on in Rome, see 7:12), "the God of heaven will set up a kingdom that shall never be destroyed" (2:44). Historically, this all works out as Christ appears and sets up His kingdom during the time that Rome rules.

Daniel 7 is an expansion of Daniel 2, with the four kingdoms represented by animals, rather than parts of a statute.

Statue of Daniel 2	Kingdom Represented	Beasts of Daniel 7
Head of Gold	Babylonia	Lion with wings of eagle
Chests and arms of silver	Medo-Persia	Bear raised up on its sides
Belly and thighs of bronze	Macedonia/Greece	Leopard with four wings and four heads
Legs of iron, feet of iron and clay	Rome	Terrifying beast with eleven horns
Stone cut without hands	Kingdom of Jesus	

Rome is presented as a beast that is "terrifying and dreadful and exceedingly strong" (v. 7). At this point, we're introduced to the eleventh horn. We're told the beast has eleven horns, which Daniel is informed are rulers who will come from this kingdom (v. 24). The eleventh king "will speak against the Most High and oppress his holy people" (v. 25 NIV). Domitian was the eleventh emperor of Rome and did these things.

Before we leave Daniel 7, we should note that there is a curious aspect to this vision. The eleventh horn uproots three of the other horns (vv. 8, 20, 24). Of course, this didn't historically happen; Roman emperors ruled until they either died or were assassinated (there were no retirement plans or parties), so Domitian couldn't have killed the emperors before him. His predecessor was his brother, Titus, who died from a fever, and Titus' predecessor was their father, Vespasian, who also died from natural causes. But what the subtraction of three horns does is figuratively move Domitian from the eleventh horn to the eighth.

It's a common practice in construction to "remove" the thirteenth floor from a building by calling it the fourteenth. They don't actually get rid of it—its designation is changed in the interest of accuracy—not numerical accuracy, but to accurately reflect the perception they want people to have of the floor (i.e., that nothing superstitious is to be associated with it). In a similar way, Domitian is moved from the eleventh to the eighth king in the interest of accuracy—not historical accuracy, but as we'll see in the next piece, there's something about being the eighth king that fits his character and describes him more completely.

QUESTIONS

1. Nebuchadnezzar has a dream about four kingdoms in Daniel 2. According to v. 44, what happens in the time of the fourth kingdom?
2. In Daniel 7, we see a terrifying beast with eleven horns. What does Daniel tell us the horns represent (v. 24)?
3. Who was the eleventh emperor of Rome? How does he become an eighth horn in Daniel's vision?

FOLLOW THE HORN, PART 2

"And I saw a beast rising out of the sea, with ten horns and seven heads, with ten diadems on its horns and blasphemous names on its heads. One of its heads seemed to have a mortal wound, but its mortal wound was healed, and the whole earth marveled as they followed the beast" (13:1, 3).

In many ways, Revelation is the New Testament sequel to Daniel. We know this because in Revelation 13, John sees a beast coming out of the sea. The beast is a composite of the four beasts mentioned in Daniel 7. We've already said something about the previous kingdoms living on in Rome, and that seems to be in view here. When Daniel lists the beasts, he gives them in the order in which they would historically appear. When John describes them, he reverses Daniel's order since he is looking backward, rather than forward (McGuiggan).

The beast has seven heads. We learn in 17:9-10 that the seven heads represent seven kings (emperors). John draws our attention to one of the heads/emperors that "seemed to have had a fatal wound, but the fatal wound had been healed" (13:3 NIV).

This is a picture of resurrection (see 5:6, where we're given a similar description in reference to Jesus). While Jesus' resurrection was literal and physical, John isn't alluding to such a thing here. Instead, this figure suggests another (eighth) emperor who parallels a previous emperor in some important way so that he is regarded as a "resurrection" of him. If we look at the emperors preceding Domitian, keeping in mind the context of Revelation (the oppression of disciples by the beast/Rome), there is an obvious candidate: Nero. He is the only one of the emperors before Domitian who persecuted the church.

Many ancient writers linked Nero and Domitian. Tertullian, a leader in the church who wrote early in the third century, calls Domitian "a limb of the bloody Nero." Eusebius, who occupied a similar role as Tertullian and lived about a century later, writes that Domitian is "the successor of Nero's campaign of hostility against God." Nero "lived on" in Domitian, just as the previous ungodly kingdoms lived on in Rome.

This is why Daniel and John make Domitian the number eight. Eight represents a new beginning/resurrection. The eighth day begins a new week. Jesus rose on the eighth day, so we have a resurrection on the day of new beginning. After seven Sabbath years came the Jubilee, when the land was restored to its original owners and debts were cancelled. Many of the early baptisteries were eight-sided to stress the new beginning/resurrection that took place at baptism. When Domitian moves against the church, it's as if Nero has been resurrected and has a new beginning in him.

That brings us to Revelation 17. Here, there's no veiled reference to an eighth king as in Revelation 13. After we're told that the beast has seven heads representing seven mountains and seven kings (vv. 9-10), John brings an eighth king into the picture in v. 11.

We're told three times that the beast, represented in the eighth king (v. 11), "once was, now is not, and yet will come" (twice in v. 8 NIV, once in v. 11 NIV). With this, John is presenting the same truth about Domitian that he previously shared in Revelation 13 and is touched on in Daniel 7. The persecuting beast once was in the time of Nero, presently is not, and yet will come when Domitian comes to power. Once again, we see Domitian aligned with Nero.

We also learn the approximate date of John's vision from this section (Henry Swete, *Commentary on Revelation*). Revelation 17:10 speaks of the seven kings preceding Domitian when it tells us, "Five have fallen, one is, the other has not yet come; but when he does come, he must remain for only a little while" (NIV). The king who "must remain for only a little while" is Domitian's brother and predecessor, Titus, who reigns for just two years. He is the seventh king. That means the one who "is" (i.e., currently reigning), is Vespasian, the father of Titus and Domitian. He is the sixth king and rules from A.D. 69-79. John is receiving this vision sometime during his reign, probably during the latter part (Swete).

So what have we seen? We've seen the Roman emperor Domitian viewed as an eleventh horn who becomes an eighth horn (Daniel 7), a head that appears to have a fatal wound but has been healed (Revelation 13), and as the beast that once was, is not, and is yet to come (Revelation 17). In all of these pictures, Daniel and John do the same thing—they portray Domitian as a resurrection of Nero in terms of his oppression of God's people.[1]

QUESTIONS

1. What is the significance of having Domitian end up as an eighth king?
2. How does "once was, now is not, and is yet to come," fit into this?
3. When was Revelation written?

---

1. I'm indebted to Jim McGuiggan's commentary on *Revelation* not only for much of my understanding of the book, but especially chapters 13 and 17. While most commentators acknowledge some connection between Daniel and Revelation, he understands the symbiotic relationship between the two.

RUNNING WITH PATIENT ENDURANCE

***"Here is a call for the endurance and faith of the saints"* (13:10).**

Stephen Kiprotich and Usain Bolt—what's the difference between these two? Well, Google Kiprotich, and at the time of this writing, you get a few hundred thousand results. Nothing shabby about that, but do the same with Bolt, and you get more than ten times that amount. Bolt is the reigning Olympic gold medalist in the 100 and 200 meter sprints. Who is Kiprotich? He's the current gold medal holder in the marathon.

While everyone has heard of Usain Bolt, hardly anyone knows Kiprotich. I suppose there are lots of reasons for that, but I want to suggest one that you probably haven't thought about: Bolt is a sprinter, while Kiprotich is a long distance runner. All other things being equal, we gravitate toward the sprint and sprinters more than we do long distance runners.

Why? Sprint is a glamour event. We watch it live, and then in replays, from different angles, in slow motion, and even with the runner commenting on it. The marathon? Well, we watch the start, and then the network goes to commercial because who wants to watch a bunch of runners putting one foot in front of the other for two-and-a-half hours? The winner might get interviewed, but don't hold your breath on it. The sprint is a high wire spectacle; the marathon is low-wattage grinding. The sprint provides us with instant gratification; the marathon requires a much longer attention span. Both events require talent, high levels of training, and plenty of tenacity. But only one really grabs our attention.

Maybe all of this explains why the quality of patient endurance never makes the spiritual talk-show circuit. You can always hear about the sprinters (love, joy, peace, hope), but very rarely is anything said about the long distance runner (patient endurance). After all, there's nothing glamorous about it; it's just putting one foot in front of the other.

But actually, that's the point. Patient endurance is about putting one foot in front of the other day after day. Whether the terrain is steep and demanding, flat and boring, or downhill and challenging—the runner keeps running. The weather might be hot, cold, humid, sunny, overcast, or raining—the runner keeps running. There might be a pack of other runners around, just a few, or absolutely no one—the runner keeps running. Progress is made, and character is measured with each step.

Revelation 13 begins with a description of a terrible beast that blasphemes God and is given power to "make war on the saints and to conquer them" (v. 7). As we've seen, the beast is a reference to Domitian and Rome and the difficulties (and in some cases, death) that would come to the followers of Christ. Although these actions would sow the seeds of their demise, this wouldn't happen before troubled times came upon the church.

"This calls for patient endurance and faithfulness on the part of God's people" (v. 10 NIV). How difficult of a message this was for our first-century family! Yet they practiced patient endurance, knowing that God was in control, their suffering wasn't without meaning, and that God would right all wrongs. Twenty centuries later, Rome is a city in Italy, and the little kingdom they were part of covers the globe!

Who knows the debt we owe to those who stood for Christ regardless of the cost? By their courageous suffering, they not only conquered—they inspired others to live for Him. Patient endurance might not get the headlines, but it's hard to argue with its results!

What is it we need to endure patiently for the cause of Christ?

QUESTIONS

1. Who or what comes to your mind when you think about patient endurance?
2. Who do you think might benefit from your patient endurance?

DISCERNMENT & DARING

***"Then I saw another beast rising out of the earth. It had two horns like a lamb and it spoke like a dragon"* (13:11).**

John sees a second beast (as if the first one wasn't enough!). Whereas the previous creature comes out of the sea, this one rises from the earth. A couple of things are clear in regard to this beast. First, he is closely connected with the sea beast. We learn in v. 12, "He exercised all of the authority of the first beast on his behalf" (NIV) so he works for and by the authority of the beast from the sea.

We're also told in the remainder of the verse that his goal is to make "the earth and its inhabitants worship the first beast." Consequently, we see the earth beast employ deception ("great signs" v. 13) in making an image of the sea beast speak (v. 15). He also uses violence—those refusing to worship the image are put to death (v. 15). Verses 16-17 suggest economic pressures are also brought to bear.

The first beast has been identified as representing Rome. It symbolizes Rome as a cruel and violent empire bent on world domination. In Daniel's words, it is "terrifying and dreadful and exceedingly strong" (7:7). The second beast is also Rome, but from a religious perspective. It has the appearance of a lamb, but the chilling voice of a dragon (v. 11). It uses religion, not to reach up to the one God, but to build and secure its empire.

We've previously discussed Asia's eagerness in embracing the imperial cult as reflected in the Temple of the Sebastoi (p. 54). Furthermore, Ephesus was known as the guardian (*neokoron*) of the god Artemis (Acts 19:35 NIV) and the god Domitian (Friesen). In light of this, it's not difficult to see the beast of the earth as a representative of the religious structures of Rome in Asia that promoted the worship of Domitian.

Publicly, there are temples, altars, coins, and statutes promoting Rome in a religious sense. Professionally, trade guilds and labor associations engage in some form of emperor worship in addition to their patron gods. Personally, homes are filled with shrines and altars. The beast is everywhere and touches every aspect of life.

For the disciple, it is a challenge to be discerning and daring. They are to "honor the emperor" (1 Peter 2:17), but at the same time, "Worship the Lord your God and him only shall you serve" (Matthew 4:10). This second command qualifies the first, and without its observance, compromise, idolatry, and immorality could easily seep in. If you think about what Christ has to say to the seven churches, almost all His admonitions deal with these three areas.

Though we live twenty centuries later in a democracy where there is a separation of church and state, compromise, idolatry (admittedly of a different sort), and immorality are still besetting sins. It is not the heavy hand of government, but popular culture, that looms over us with its own version of distractions, deceptions, and discouragements. We don't face terrorizing beasts as much as pleasure and comforts that incrementally move us away from a passionate pursuit of Jesus and His kingdom. May we be blessed with the discernment and daring to follow Him who is our Hope!

QUESTIONS

1. What evidence is there to suggest that the second beast represents Rome from a religious perspective? How was religion an instrument of the state?
2. In what ways did Christians of this time need to be discerning and daring? In what ways do we need to do the same thing today?

FAQ

Who is standing on the shore at the beginning of Revelation 13—the dragon or John?

This question arises because some manuscripts say "and I," rather than "the dragon." The better manuscripts have "the dragon." Contextually, either reading would work. If it's John, then he's getting an up-close and personal view of the beast as it emerges from the sea. If it's the dragon, then he's overseeing the evil that is being brought by the two beasts. Like most variant readings, either one is possible and doesn't affect how we understand John's vision.

Wasn't Julius Caesar the first emperor of Rome?

Most historians recognize Augustus as the first emperor of the Roman Empire. Prior to him, Rome existed as a republic. In the century before Augustus, that republic was in constant turmoil often resulting in civil war. Leaders such as Marius, Sulla, Caesar, Pompey, and Mark Antony all contributed to this weakening. And although Julius Caesar is the most well-known of these, he was neither the first nor the last to assume dictatorial powers. After Caesar's assassination, there was another decade of civil war before Augustus was able to consolidate power and become emperor.

Some are under the impression that since most of the emperors have "Caesar" in their titles, this is evidence that Julius Caesar was the first emperor. It's not. Augustus was Caesar's great nephew and became his legally adopted son and heir according to the provisions of Caesar's will after his assassination (Caesar had no son of his own). By taking his name, Augustus was simply co-opting his great uncle's legacy (i.e., his name and wealth), to his political advantage. Like many who die in office, Caesar became more popular in death than life. He was the first public official to be deified. Emperors after Augustus followed suit and took the name to enhance their reputation.

One of the seven heads of the beast that John sees seems to have a fatal wound that has been healed (13:1, 3). How do you get an eighth king from this? If it's a resurrection, then wouldn't it still have to be the seventh king who's resurrected? After all, Jesus is the Lamb that looked as if it had been slain (5:6), and there's only "one" of Him.

This makes a lot of sense if you're in a book of literal speech, but we're not. And granted, if we had to make the case for an eighth king from Revelation 13 alone, it would be more difficult. However, 17:10-11 specifically mentions an eighth king who "belongs to the seven." So the head that seems to have a fatal wound does indeed represent two rulers (Nero and Domitian). They are paired because they were both oppressors of the church and as such, Domitian appears to be the "resurrection" of Nero.

Who are the seven kings (emperors) before Domitian (17:10ff)?

Historically, of course, there are ten emperors before Domitian

(Daniel 7:24ff). He is the eleventh and is pictured as subduing three kings so that, image-wise, he can become number eight (vv. 8, 24). Eight is the number of new beginning/resurrection, and this speaks to Domitian as the resurrection of Nero—the only one of the previous emperors to persecute the church.

In Revelation 13 and 17, John simply takes up where Daniel leaves off—with eight kings. The seven who come before Domitian (17:10) would include Nero, Vespasian, and Titus, since they are all referred to by John (Nero by implication and Vespasian and Titus in v. 10). After that, it really doesn't matter who the other four kings are any more than it matters who the three are that were subdued. Whoever we might choose would fit the role of being part of the Roman beast that is covered with blasphemous names (v. 3).

Doesn't "666" refer to Nero? According to gematria (the practice of assigning numerical values to letters and significance to the sum of the letters in a word), Nero = 666.

This is one of those little bits of information that seemingly everyone has heard (and many have embraced). It's the kind of thing that make us "oooh" and "aaah" as it suggests that someone has broken the mysterious divine code as they shine a flashlight on their face in the dark and tell us that when numerical values are assigned to the word "Nero," it comes out to "666."

While it is true that you can take NRWN QSR (the Hebrew for Nero Caesar), assign numerical values to each letter, and come up with 666; it is also true that you can do the same thing for Domitian, Adolph Hitler, Bill Clinton, etc. (Michael Gorman, *Reading Revelation Responsibly*). David Aune (*Revelation*) shares Stauffer's finding that an abbreviated official title of Domitian found on some coins equals 666. All of this brings out the point that one of the challenges of gemetria is determining exactly how and what values should be assigned to each letter.

It also points us to the context of Revelation, rather than an ancient, ambiguous, symbolic, numeric system in order to determine the meaning of 666. Nero as the beast simply doesn't fit Revelation or Daniel 7 (there's no way he's the eleventh emperor of Rome).

What does 666 mean? It is a parody of perfection (777), and aptly describes the beast. The beast is a satanic imitation of the Lamb. Christ's followers are marked (7:3ff), and so are the beast's (13:16-17). Jesus was alive, then died, and now is alive again, and so is the beast who "once was, now is not, and yet will come" (17:8 NIV). Christ was resurrected on the eighth day (the first day of the week), so the beast is an "eighth" king (17:11).

This is why the number of the beast is 666. It is an imitation, but it falls short. It is not 777, the number of fullness and perfection. It is the number of man, not God (13:18). Again, we see the difference between appearance and reality.

ALL OVER THIS LAND

***"Then I looked, and behold, on Mount Zion stood the Lamb, and with him 144,000 who had his name and his Father's name written on their foreheads"* (14:1).**

In 1949, Pete Seeger and Lee Hays wrote a protest song of sorts called "If I Had a Hammer." Over the years, the song was reworked by different artists, and in 1962, it resurfaced in its most familiar form on the debut album of a trio known only by their first names—Peter, Paul & Mary. Since that time, the song has been co-opted by different groups for different purposes, the most notable being the Civil Rights Movement. The third verse of the song has these words:

If I had a song, I'd sing it in the morning,
I'd sing it in the evening, all over this land.
I'd sing out danger, I'd sing out a warning,
I'd sing out love between my brothers and my sisters
All over this land.

This verse really grabs us if we think about all of the people down through the centuries who have suffered with nothing but a song in their hearts to sustain them. Music is powerful in that way, isn't it? There's something in a song that supplies inspiration, yet at the same time defies explanation. Maybe that's why it's so sad when someone loses their song.

In the preceding chapter, we saw John present a terrifying picture involving a dragon (Satan) and two hideous beasts, one from the sea and one from the earth. The beast from the sea curses God and makes war against the followers of Jesus (13:5, 7), while the second beast works in concert as it compels all who are not followers of the Lamb to worship the first beast.

Juxtaposed with this horrific vision is the picture of Revelation 14. There the Lamb stands on Mount Zion with 144,000 followers. As previously noted, this number represents fullness and completeness. How many of the Lamb's followers are lost to the beasts? Zero. Zip. Nada. And what are they doing there on Mount Zion with Jesus? Well, they're singing their song.

It's a "new" song. In the Scripture, a "new" song is one that celebrates some new aspect of God's love and care (Psalm 40:1-3; 98:1ff; Isaiah 42:8-9; 43:18-19). And notice that the only people capable of singing the song are those who have been redeemed (v. 3). You can't name it if you don't claim it.

The church has a song to sing! It is a song of protest against evil and injustice, but it's more than that. It's a song of hope and victory through the Lamb. It will sustain us in our darkest night, as well as remind us on our brightest day that our strength is in Him. No one else can sing this song, so if we don't, it won't be heard! That would be a shame because it's a great song, and everyone should have the chance to hear it.

All over this land.

QUESTIONS

1. How does 14:1-5 stand in contrast to the two beasts of Revelation 13?
2. In Scripture, what is a "new song?" Who can sing it?
3. Why is it so important that followers of the Lamb never stop singing their song?

WORKING OR WILTING

"And I heard a voice from heaven saying, 'Write this: Blessed are the dead who die in the Lord from now on.' 'Blessed indeed,' says the Spirit, 'that they may rest from their labors, for their deeds follow them!'" (14:13).

In developing what happens in connection with the sounding of the seventh trumpet and the ultimate judgment it brings upon Rome, we've seen Satan (the dragon) make three efforts against God and go down to defeat on all three occasions (Revelation 12). Then we were shown two horrific beasts under the dragon's control (in 13:1, the better manuscripts have him standing on the shore of the sea, so that what follows is of his doing). The second beast compels the inhabitants of the earth to worship the first beast (v. 12). They receive a mark of the beast that enables them to participate in commerce (vv. 16-17). All of this is in vain, as it turns out, because we see a vision of the triumphant Lamb in the next chapter with all of His people standing on Mount Zion, wearing their own mark (14:1).

Three angels now appear to communicate in verbal form the message we've been seeing through images. The first angel reminds us that the time of judgment has come (v. 7). The second angel speaks of Babylon (Rome) as fallen and indicts her for intoxicating the nations with her adulteries (v. 8 NIV, i.e., commercial alliances). The third angel speaks judgment to those who worship the beast and his image (vv. 9-11). By the mouth of two or three witnesses, everything has been confirmed.

In contrast to this, a blessing is pronounced on the dead who die in the Lord (v. 13). The Spirit agrees and adds "they will rest from their labor, for their deeds will follow them" (v. 13 NIV). I'm sure one of the truths John's readers are to see in this is that death in the Lord is superior to life without Him, for some of them would be forced to act upon their belief in regard to this.

Beyond that though, it also says something to those who are practicing patient endurance (v. 12 NIV). Anything that involves endurance isn't easy, and continuing in the conflict and opposition these churches were experiencing had to be extremely difficult. In such cases, choosing to practice the will of God became the path of much resistance. They had the choice of working or wilting, and they chose to work!

In the end, isn't that the way it works out for all of us? Sooner or later, don't we all encounter obstacles in following Christ? Maybe it's the challenge to love someone who is hateful towards us. It might be resisting something that strongly tempts us. Or perhaps it's practicing humility in front of the arrogant. Obstacles come in all shapes, sizes, and degrees, but in the end they usually demand the same thing of us—that we intensify our efforts.

To do this consistently is to practice patient endurance, and we're assured here of two things: rest and remembrance. Death will bring a cessation of the need for these labors, and "their deeds will follow them." What we do in this life might have been a secret on earth, but not in heaven. And it's worth noting that we're not talking about a few, or some, or even most of our actions. "Their deeds"—the entire collection—will be on display.

All of this encourages disciples then and now to continue the work of being faithful witnesses.

QUESTIONS

1. What do the three angels say? How is it alike? Different?
2. How do vv. 12-13 challenge disciples? How does it assure them?

FAQ

It's obvious that the 144,000 represent the totality of God's people being delivered. Why are they said to be virgins "who did not defile themselves with women"?

By this juncture, we've learned to look at figurative speech like this and ask the question, "What truth is this meant to convey?" Since John tells us that the 144,000 "follow the Lamb wherever he goes" (v. 4) and are "blameless" (v. 5), it seems that the sexual metaphor is brought in to emphasize their faithfulness to the Lamb in the face of strong temptation. The disciples are displaying commitment like that of an unmarried man keeping himself sexually pure in the midst of an immoral culture—an image that powerfully resonates in our own culture with its host of sexual temptations.

What are the harvest and winepress at the end of the chapter meant to convey?

I think they have to do with the preservation of the righteous and punishment of the wicked. We've seen this theme throughout Revelation, and here the harvest is of the righteous, while the trampling of the grapes in "the great winepress of God's wrath" (v. 19 NIV) has to do with the ungodly. We see something of this same kind of thing in Matthew 13:36-43, though I understand Jesus there to be speaking of the judgment brought upon the unbelieving Jews in A.D. 70.

What have we seen?

As we move toward Rome's ultimate judgment, disciples have received complete assurance by seeing Satan defeated three times (Revelation 12). This being so, we know that the two beasts that align themselves with him, though fierce and gruesome (Revelation 13), will go down to defeat as well. While the wicked are defeated, the righteous (as has been the constant theme of the book) are brought through it all and sing their song of deliverance (Revelation 14). This deliverance is pictured in the harvesting of the earth, while the three angels speak against the wicked who are thrown into the winepress of God's wrath.

PART SIX

Judgment Day for Rome

It's time for judgment on Domitian and Rome. The whole book has been building up to the coming of Christ in judgment upon the Empire (1:7), but especially since Jesus started taking the seals off the scroll in Revelation 6. We've seen the seals reveal, we've heard the trumpets warn, and now it's time for the bowls of wrath to be poured out. What transpires isn't hard to follow.

The scene in heaven (15)
The pouring out of the bowls (16)
A closer look at Rome (17-18)
Judgment of two beasts and Satan (19-20)

GETTING LOST IN THE GLORY OF GOD

"Standing beside the sea of glass with harps of God in their hands. And they sing the song of Moses, the servant of God, and the song of the Lamb" (15:2-3).

In 15:1, John sees another sign in heaven: it's the seven angels with the final plagues. They are the last "because with them God's wrath is completed" (NIV). He sees the sea (where the beast had been) on fire. Beside the sea are those who have been victorious. The scene is reminiscent of Israel beside the Red Sea after Pharaoh and his army had been engulfed by its waters (Exodus 14).

It's not surprising that we are told that those who have overcome are singing a song of Moses and the Lamb (v. 3). This is the same thing as the "new song" they were said to be singing in 14:3. It celebrates their rescue from Rome, just as Moses' song commemorated Israel's escape from Egypt (Exodus 15). It is a song of the Lamb because their deliverance comes through Him, and there is no finer song to sing on earth or in heaven.

We've seen this type of scene (celebration before the throne of God) throughout Revelation (chapters 4-5, 7, 14, etc.), so you could say it's normative to the book. What we see in these scenes conveys the essence of worship—getting lost in the glory of God. What we hear in such scenes reflects this. Let's listen in.

"Great and amazing are your deeds, O Lord God the Almighty!" This is what people who have experienced victory say (v. 2). There's no confusion as to the reason, and they want everyone to know: it is the Lord God Almighty.

"Just and true are your ways, O King of the nations!" Maybe it didn't always seem this way, but now they have no doubts. It's true that, right now, we may wonder and even question God as the psalmists sometimes did, but a day is coming when we will question no more. In the meantime, we'll do well to doubt our doubts rather than our Father.

"Who will not fear, O Lord, and glorify your name?" The question is rhetorical, but in the book, we do see those who, though given every opportunity to repent, refuse to do so. Their fate is made clear, and it's not an option worth considering.

"For you alone are holy. All nations will come and worship you, for your righteous acts have been revealed." The King of the nations will receive the honor that belongs to Him!

The adage "you become what you worship" really is true (Psalm 115:4-8; 135:15-18). Israel "followed worthless idols and themselves became worthless" (2 Kings 17:15 NIV). Worship things, and we end up greedy and covetous. Worship status, and we become prideful. Worship self, and we end up narcissistic. When we worship God, we are transformed into His image. We were created in His image, and worship brings us back to where we belong.

We'll never possess a greater sense of hope than when we get lost in His glory.

QUESTIONS

1. It is suggested that the essence of worship is getting lost in the glory of God. What does this mean to you? Can you think of times when this has been your experience?
2. How is it that "worship brings us back where we belong"?

WHEN THERE IS NO HOPE

"Out of the sanctuary came the seven angels with the seven plagues, clothed in pure, bright linen, with golden sashes around their chests. And one of the four living creatures gave to the seven angels seven golden bowls full of the wrath of God who lives forever and ever" (15:6-7).

We've talked about the seals, trumpets, and bowls being like a nesting doll: when we open one it leads to another. We saw the opening of the seventh seal reveal the seven trumpets (8:1-2). In the same way, the sounding of the seventh trumpet leads to the pouring out of the seven bowls of wrath. It's easy to miss this, though, because while we're told back in 11:15 that the seventh trumpet sounded, it's not until 15:7-8 that we actually hear of the seven bowls of wrath. That's a considerable interim in which John has seen the woman, dragon, and child (Revelation 12), the two beasts (13), the 144,000, three angels, the harvest and the winepress (14), and finally back to Heaven again (the first part of 15). In fact, this interim begins and ends with a great sign in Heaven (12:1; 15:1).

In one sense, it's all quite dizzying in its effect. But John has simply been doing what any storyteller does: building toward the climax by offering new images that reinforce his basic theme of salvation and judgment. What helps us to see the connection between the seventh trumpet and the seven bowls is the temple imagery that is associated with both. In 11:15, the seventh angel sounds his trumpet, God's temple in heaven is opened, and the Ark of the Covenant is in view (v. 19). In 15:1, we have the angels with the seven plagues (bowls, vv. 7-8), and John sees in heaven "the tabernacle of the covenant law" and it is open, implying the Ark is visible (v. 5).

The point of this imagery is to make it clear that judgment is the holy response of God. Unlike the Greco-Roman gods, God is not temperamental or arbitrary in His judgments. They proceed from His holy character. Moreover, Rome's wickedness is not superficial or peripheral; their deeds have violated the heart of what is good, right, and true. Judgment now proceeds, not from the outer courts, but from the innermost part of the temple. The seven angels come out from His presence dressed in priestly clothing (v. 6). One of the four living creatures gives to them the seven bowls "filled with the wrath of God" (v. 7 NIV). The last thing we're told is that the smoke from God's glory and power is such that no one can enter the temple until judgment is completed (v. 8). God's judgment is as irreversible as it is awesome.

Most of us have some experience with situations where there was no longer any hope of physical life continuing. When it's someone who has lived a long life and been in diminishing health, I suppose it is "easier" in some sense, and, like me, you might have known people in such situations who were ready to go. But when it's someone who's relatively young, and they've been told that there's no longer any hope, the treatments aren't working, and there is nothing else left to try, it's like the extinguishing of all light. I've experienced the loss of a couple of friends this way and vividly remember the sadness on these occasions. I'm glad to say that both of them belonged to Jesus, so that even when their hope of physical life was gone, they (and we) took great comfort in knowing they were going to be with God. I can't imagine what it's like to have no hope of any kind, as the text speaks of here.

To live in rebellion to God is to be headed in the direction of no hope. No matter what anyone might think, no one really has an idea of what that is like. I'm not thinking now of the punitive aspect; I'm speaking of the crushing sense of disappointment that will be experienced when it is realized that the precious gift of life was squandered by living in some way other than in service to God.

No hope is no way to live or die.

QUESTIONS

1. What is the significance of the temple imagery? How had Rome violated God's holiness?
2. Rome's impenitence led to judgment that was "as irreversible as it was awesome." What is God's attitude toward people who live penitently (1 John 1:8-10)?

THE JUDGE OF THE EARTH WILL DO WHAT IS RIGHT

"And I heard the altar saying, 'Yes, Lord God the Almighty, true and just are your judgments!'" (16:7).

A voice from the temple instructs the seven angels to pour out the bowls of God's wrath upon the earth. Like the trumpets, the judgments that follow bear many similarities to what God did against Egypt in the plagues leading to the exodus. Like the trumpets, I don't think we're meant to literalize these; they simply speak to the wrath of God that is about to come on Rome. Unlike the trumpets, which were partial judgments in order to bring about repentance, there is nothing partial about these because repentance is no longer an option. They are apparently past the point where it is even possible (vv. 9, 11).

The first bowl marks with festering sores those who bear the mark of the beast. The second and third strike all of the waters, turning them into blood. The angel in charge of the waters testifies to the justness of this since they were responsible for shedding the blood of God's people. The altar, under which are those who sacrificed their lives (6:9), answers back in agreement. Abraham's question from Genesis 18:25, "Will not the Judge of all the earth do right?" (NIV) is answered (again) in Revelation. God will do what is right!

Among other things, it's confidence in our Father's righteousness that inspires right living in us. Because we are assured that His might promotes right, we know that nothing we do in heaven's direction is in vain. All of our efforts count, regardless of how they might appear to have turned out on earth. If no wrong goes unpunished (as we see here), then it's also true that no right goes unrewarded!

This is something we need to hold in our heart and remind each other of regularly. We live in a culture of pagan pragmatism where ideals are often sacrificed on the altar of results. What will "get us ahead" is worshipped, and what "doesn't work" is jettisoned. The Labans of the world are fêted, while the righteous are often ridiculed. We need to see the end from the beginning and know that doing right is never wrong.

I knew a man whose business partner liquidated the company's assets and then disappeared (along with the woman who kept the books). They had apparently been planning their crime for some time and left numerous bills unpaid in order to maximize the amount they could steal. This left the man and a third partner responsible for a large amount of debt. By the time the couple was tracked down, they were living on the other side of the country and had spent most of the money setting up their retirement. Since he owned 51% of the company, and all of the books were gone, the other two partners faced an uphill legal battle to recover their losses and pay their bills. Everyone urged them to declare bankruptcy. The man didn't think that was the honorable course of action, so he worked past his planned retirement age to pay off the debts. Of course, the whole affair wiped out the nice retirement he had planned for himself and his wife.

He's gone on to be with the Lord. Do you suppose he regrets for a moment the sacrifices he made in order to do what was right? Do you think there's any chance these things went unnoticed by our Father? The justness of God that this text points to assures us that they were not.

Our hope hangs on the truth that the Judge of the earth will do what is right.

QUESTIONS

1. How often do you think about God's righteousness? How much of an impact does it have on your actions?
2. Confidence in God's righteousness inspires right living on our part. What are some other things that motivate us to do what is right?

THE BATTLE OF ARMAGEDDON, PART 1

***"And they assembled them at the place that in Hebrew is called Armageddon"* (16:16).**

Almost everyone has heard of the Battle of Armageddon, right? And that's part of the problem. What they've usually heard are lots of different things from several different sources, so that the end result is often not clarity, but confusion—and quite a bit of it. Kept in its context, we'll see that the Battle of Armageddon is neither the end of the world nor the return of Jesus. It is yet another way that John has of describing the judgment on Rome. And in a chapter where there are 100-pound hailstones falling from the sky, the sun scorching people with fire, and a city being split into three parts by an earthquake—the kings of the earth gathering for battle fits right in.

Armageddon (literally, "hill of Megiddo") is spoken of only in Revelation 16:16. There the kings of the earth are brought together by the dragon, the beast, and the false prophet "for battle on the great day of God the Almighty." (v. 14). After this, we are told, "Look, I come like a thief! Blessed is the one who stays awake and remains clothed, so as not to go naked and be shamefully exposed" (v. 15 NIV). So we have "the great day of God the Almighty" followed by the promise of a divine visitation.

It's not hard to see how literalizing this will result in understanding it as speaking of the end of the world. However, phrases like "day of the Lord" or "coming of the Lord" don't always refer to an event at the end of time; the meaning of these phrases varies according to context. Isaiah speaks against Babylon in 13:1ff. The "day of the Lord" he mentions in v. 6 and v. 9 has to do with Babylon's overthrow by the Medes (v. 17). Since God is ultimately the One who brings this about, it makes sense to refer to it as the "day of the Lord." We see this same type of usage with other prophets as well (Zephaniah 1:4, 7-8, 14, 18; 2:2-3; Malachi 4:5).

This same thing is also true for the word "coming." Isaiah 19:1 (NIV) speaks of God coming to Egypt. Then there's Micah 1:1,3, and how about the "coming" James speaks of in 5:7-9? Since it is said to be "near" in James' day (v. 8 NIV), it would be hard to understand this as the return of Jesus at the end of time.

All of this reminds us that we must be careful not to import a preconceived meaning into the text. Instead, we need to determine the meaning of a word or phrase by the context in which it occurs. We recognize this principle in our communication with others, and it keeps us from jumping to unwarranted conclusions.

For example, I purchased a Jaguar a few years ago. Maybe it was a mid-life crisis—I'm not sure. I didn't take it to church on Sundays or Wednesday nights, so most of the members weren't aware that I had it. At home, I always put it in the garage—I never left it in the driveway. To tell the truth at my height (6' 3"), I was a little too big for it, and after a while, I realized I needed to do something with it. So I gave it to our youngest daughter.

You do understand I'm talking about a Schwinn Jaguar bicycle, don't you?

And that's the way it works. Rather than automatically assign a meaning to a word or phrase, we must carefully work with the context to determine how it is being used.

QUESTIONS

1. What are some of the phrases in Revelation 16 that lead people to think the Battle of Armageddon will occur at the end of time? How do we know these phrases can be understood in other ways?
2. Can you think of some commonly used words that have to be defined by their context?

THE BATTLE OF ARMAGEDDON, PART 2

We've shown that there is nothing inherent in either the context of Revelation 16:16ff, the phrase "the great day of God Almighty" or the word "coming" that necessitate us understanding this text to be speaking of the end of the world/return of Jesus. What then is it speaking of?

The dragon, the beast, and the false prophet are images introduced to us earlier in Revelation 12-13. The dragon is clearly a figure of Satan, while the beast and false prophet are representations of Rome. In Revelation 13, remember that there are actually two beasts. But the second beast acts as a false prophet as it deceives the inhabitants of the earth (v. 14) so that's how it's presented here. What John is telling us is that these three muster all of the might they can to do battle against God. That's the truth that we're to see. It serves as a prequel to the rest of the story that is found in 19:14-21.

There, John tells us that heaven opens up, and once again, we see the rider on the white horse. This is Jesus. He is spoken of in numerous ways. "His eyes are like blazing fire" (v. 12 NIV; 1:14). His name is "the Word of God" (v. 13). He is "King of kings, and Lord of lords" (v. 16). He is in full attack mode, and He has the armies of heaven behind Him. An angel cries out to the birds to ready themselves to feast on the flesh of those who are about to fall. If you're an enemy of God, this is ominous!

No details of the battle are given because apparently there aren't any—it's over before it begins. The beast and false prophet are captured and thrown into the fiery lake. The rest of their army is killed and devoured by the birds. It is a gruesome end, but it is just (v. 11). The swiftness of judgment and the absolute destruction of the enemies of God provide justice and, therefore, comfort to those who have suffered long and endured much.

Even though the battle is over, we're not done yet. Notice that nothing has been said of the dragon's (Satan's) demise. That's because John will deal with his fate in Revelation 20.

QUESTIONS

1. If the Battle of Armageddon isn't about the end of the world, what is it about?
2. Who defeats the beast and false prophet? How does this tie the book together?

FAQ

Who are the kings of the east (v. 12)?

I understand them to represent those who are on the Lord's side. These kings are associated with the sixth bowl, but the place to begin in understanding the sixth bowl is with the sixth trumpet (9:13ff). There, four angels who are bound at the Euphrates (v. 14) are released to kill a third of mankind (v. 15). These angels stand for armies, as the next verse tells us that the number of mounted troops is 200 million. Since the Euphrates was the boundary for the Parthians (enemies of Rome), it's possible we should understand them to be the invading force.

When we get to the pouring out of the sixth bowl, we see a similar picture. Although some have taken the kings of the east to be part of the forces gathered to battle against Jesus and His army, a better case can be made for them being allies. The fact that they come from the east not only aligns them with the Parthians, but with Jesus, the bright morning star (22:16). Moreover, the drying up of the waters is something associated with God (not Satan) and happens before the demonic spirits gather their army in v. 14.

Why is Rome referred to as Babylon?

The word "Babylon" occurs five times in Revelation. It's clustered in and around the section that speaks of Rome's economic alliances. It's introduced in 14:8 where the angel says, "Fallen! Fallen is Babylon the Great, which made all the nations drink the maddening wine of her adulteries" (NIV). This is an allusion to Jeremiah 51:7, "Babylon was a golden cup in the LORD's hand, making all the earth drunken; the nations drank of her wine; therefore the nations went mad." Just as Babylon influenced the nations of the world for evil, so does Rome. Add to this the fact that Babylon destroyed Jerusalem, as did Rome, so you have another reason for the identification.

WE'RE WITH HIM

"And the ten horns that you saw are ten kings who have not yet received royal power, but they are to receive authority as kings for one hour, together with the beast. These are of one mind, and they hand over their power and authority to the beast. They will make war on the Lamb, and the Lamb will conquer them, for he is Lord of lords and King of kings, and those with him are called and chosen and faithful" **(17:12-14).**

We've seen the bowls of wrath poured out and the Battle of Armageddon begin. What follows in the next two chapters is a cutaway look at Rome and its punishment (17:1, 18) before we return to Armageddon in Revelation 19.

John sees a great prostitute who sits by the many waters (nations, v. 15). With her, the kings of the earth commit adultery, and the inhabitants of the earth are intoxicated "with wine of her adulteries" (v. 2 NIV). The prostitute represents Rome (v. 18), this time from a commercial vantage point. Rulers engaged in economic alliances ("adulteries" NIV) with the corrupt Empire because there was money to be made (18:3, 9). Likewise, business people ("merchants of the earth") were intoxicated by the wealth these arrangements offered (18:11-19). This will be developed in greater detail in the section after the next FAQ, but it speaks to individuals and nations aligning themselves with wickedness because it was profitable.

This money-over-morality mindset is with us just as much as it was in Rome's day!

At this point, the picture morphs, and we see the woman sitting on the scarlet beast with seven heads, ten horns, and covered with blasphemous names. It's not hard to see how these symbols of power (beast, heads, and horns), suggest that Rome's political and military might are contributing factors to their expanding markets. Seduction takes place, not just because there was money to be made—there was influence to be gained and powers to be appeased.

We've discussed the seven heads earlier (pp. 149ff). They are the emperors of Rome. The ten horns John speaks of here are part of the beast (v. 3), but are also differentiated from it (vv. 12-13). For "one hour," they are empowered with Rome to wage war against the Lamb. This speaks to the client kings or sub-rulers of the Roman Empire. They were kings like Herod who ruled their lands for Rome (there's no reason to force "ten" to be literal). They obviously played an important part in terms of helping Rome stabilize its provinces, but are probably mentioned here because of the role they would play in promoting the emperor worship for which provinces like Asia were known. In doing this, they were waging war against the Lamb and His followers.

It would all prove futile of course; they were going against the Lord of lords and King of kings. We're to see in this title given to Christ more than omnipotence; it's power connected to character. Jesus has full sovereignty by virtue of the completeness of His surrender to God (5:9ff). It's not just that He's stronger than all; He is stronger because he is better. That's why He will triumph. Good is stronger than evil because it is better.

And those who belong to Him are part of the victory. They are identified as those who are "with" Him. What a wonderful designation! Someone wants to know who we are? Well, we're with Him—the One who loves us and freed us from our sins, the Ruler of the kings of the earth, the Lord of the universe. This was just the message that people with their back against the wall needed to hear. It's a message that we need as well.

It made a difference in their lives, and it will make a difference in the way we live when we think of ourselves as with Him. It will influence how we think, how we speak, where we go, and what we do if we remember it's all done with Him. Let's live like the called, the chosen, and the faithful.

Let's live with Him.

QUESTIONS

1. W hat do the ten horns represent? How were they important to Rome?
2. Those that are with Jesus are identified as called, chosen, and faithful. Why do you think these three words are used? How do they speak to our lives?

FAQ

How can the beast and the woman both represent Rome when we're told that the beast and the ten horns will hate the prostitute and bring her to ruin (v. 16)?

What symbol would you choose to represent America? Would it be the flag, the Statue of Liberty, "amber waves of grain," or perhaps a pilgrim? In the end, it would depend on what aspect of America you wanted to highlight. In the same way, throughout Revelation, Rome is presented in multiple images: a beast that's a composite of different animals (13), a beast/false prophet that has two horns like a lamb but speaks like a dragon (13, 16), Babylon (several chapters), and a prostitute (17). None of these images speak of Rome in its entirety (although Babylon might come the closest). Instead, they emphasize certain aspects of the Empire. The composite beast represents the brutality and evil of previous kingdoms now embodied in Rome. The beast/false prophet that looks like a lamb is Rome's religious side that encourages people to bow to the state. The prostitute is Rome's commercial power that seduces surrounding nations into alliances.

What's being said in v. 16ff is the same thing that is predicted in Daniel 2:33-34, 41-43. Rome's ultimate demise will come partially from within. The beast and ten kings hating the prostitute merely state this truth in a symbolic way. In this, we see the principle that wickedness and evil carry within themselves the seeds of their own destruction (Galatians 6:8).

Since the Roman Empire didn't end with the assassination of Domitian in A.D. 96, how can it be said that Rome falls with his death?

Do all wars end when the peace treaty is signed, or when one side inflicts an irreversible loss on the other that causes them to seek terms of peace? Does a retailer have their profit or loss determined at the very end of the year, or could some earlier pivotal event (like Black Friday) determine what its outcome will be? Illustrations could be multiplied, but the truth we're after is that sometimes the end is nothing more than a formality—the outcome has already been determined. I think that's the way we're to understand Rome's fall. From God's point of view, in the death of Domitian, Rome has been judged and found wanting; their end is but a formality.

This perspective is common to the Scriptures as you would expect it to be, since the writers usually speak of things from God's point of view rather than man's. Saul is rejected as king (1 Samuel 15:23) long before his end finally comes (1 Samuel 31:6). The same is true for Ahab and Jezebel (1 Kings 21:19-23; 22:29ff; 2 Kings 9:30ff). McGuiggan points out how, with the judgment of Antiochus IV Epiphanies (Daniel 8, 11), the Seleucid Empire is viewed as over, even though it remained for another century. In the same way, Rome is seen as judged and fallen with the death of Domitian.

ROME, FAITH, & FINANCES

"Then I heard another voice from heaven saying, 'Come out of her, my people, lest you take part in her sins, lest you share in her plagues'" (18:4).

In the two-chapter cutaway of Rome, we've moved from looking at the Empire (Revelation 17) to hearing about it (18). Angels, kings, merchants, and sea captains now give their testimony relative to Rome's fall. Although it continues to be spoken of primarily in commercial and economic terms, the emphasis in this section is on the greatness of Rome's collapse (the bigger they are, the harder they fall). In the midst of its demise, there is a call to disciples.

To appreciate it, we must avoid falling into the trap of thinking of persecution exclusively in ultimate (life or death) terms. It more often exists in lesser degrees: consequences here, a restriction there, intimidation, etc. This is happening to Christians in certain areas of the world today and was also taking place in the first century (Hebrews 10:32-34). Economic deprivation was a common way disciples suffered. It's not difficult to imagine how believers could be denied work, their businesses boycotted or vandalized, or how they might come into conflict with the trade guilds as Paul did in Acts 19:23ff.

If there were economic trials for followers of Christ, there were also corresponding temptations. For a shop owner, it might be selling a trinket that represented a god. Such an item would ingratiate him to the community and have the potential for substantial sales. Since he knew there was really no such god behind the idol (1 Corinthians 8:4ff), what harm was there?

Then there were the trade guilds with their patron gods. Membership in them could be crucial to finding work in one's trade, yet it would involve paying homage to a god or goddess and (likely) participation in feasts, where meat sacrificed to idols was served, and sexual temptations abounded. In short, there were lots of ways then, as now, to compromise faith for the sake of financial gain.

We shouldn't be surprised, then, to find this dealt with in Revelation as part of the overall warning to disciples to avoid compromising their faith. God's people are told to "Come out of her, my people, lest you take part in her sins" (v. 4). In Isaiah (52:11) and Jeremiah (51:6, 9, 45), this has to do with a physical departure from Babylon. The leaving that is commanded here is a spiritual one. They must detach themselves from Rome's wickedness, and the particular form under discussion is economic. They must not fall into the same trap the nations did by becoming part of a corrupt system for monetary gain.

It's possible this was an element of the Laodiceans' lukewarmness (Gorman). They were rebuked for saying, "I am rich, I have prospered, and I need nothing" (3:17). Although haughty self-sufficiency is clearly being condemned, wealth acquired through compromising faith may have also contributed to the visceral response of Jesus (v. 16).

Revelation tells us that hard times came in many forms upon the disciples. But by following the Lamb, they overcame them all!

QUESTIONS

1. In what ways were the disciples in Asia financially tempted by Rome? In what ways are disciples today tempted by our culture?
2. How can wealth be deceitful and choke off our spirituality (Matthew 13:22)? How can we guard against this?

DISCIPLED LIVES

"Then I heard another voice from heaven saying, "'Come out of her, my people, lest you take part in her sins, lest you share in her plagues'" (18:4).

In Hemingway's classic, *The Old Man and the Sea,* an elderly fisherman named Santiago hasn't caught anything in almost three months. Things are so bad that Manolin, his young apprentice, has been forbidden by his parents from fishing with him. They want him to go out with the more successful fisherman.

A dejected and desperate man, Santiago sails from his small village in Cuba, taking his boat far out in the Gulf Stream into the Florida Straits. His efforts initially pay off as he hooks a great marlin. He fights it for three days before the fish comes close enough for Santiago to harpoon it. However, as he heads back to Cuba with his magnificent catch tied to the side of his boat, sharks attack the marlin numerous times so that when he finally arrives, there is little more than a skeleton remaining. (Hemingway had such an experience years before when a thousand pound marlin he caught was attacked and about half of it was eaten before he could get back to the dock). At the time of the attacks and afterwards, Santiago chides himself saying, "I went out too far."

Most of us aren't that unlike Santiago in that we can venture out too far. In our consumer culture, it's not hard to fall into the trap of excess—thinking that if a little of something is good, then boatloads of it will be wonderful. Yet the moment we begin to define ourselves by what we have (as advertisers are constantly encouraging us to do), we have gone out too far. We might end up with everything to live with, but if we have nothing to live for, it is meaningless—a skeleton of what our Father intended life to be.

The same is true in regard to ambition and achievement. While these are normally good attributes, we can go out too far if they skew our priorities and become our reason for living. We've all seen too many examples of people who were so driven in this regard that they devalued their marriages or their families in order to "get ahead." God must remain at our center, or we become eccentric in a way that is unhealthy.

At the other end of the spectrum are those who adopt the Disneyland approach to life. Everything has to be fun—so they glut themselves with beyond-their-budget vacations, non-stop entertainment, and an all-consuming quest for the next big thrill to post on Facebook or tweet about on Twitter. Life is not about improvement but indulgence. They also have gone out too far.

It was Gordon Dahl who several years ago made the famous observation that Americans tend to "to worship their work, to work at their play, and to play at their worship." I'm not sure that I know many people for whom all three of these things are true, but I know many (myself included) who struggle with at least one of these areas.

Balanced lives aren't easy because they require discipline. Discipline doesn't come naturally for most of us; it occurs only when core faith convictions become embedded in our behavior to the point that we exercise self-restraint. This keeps us from going out too far and ending up with a skeleton instead of a life.

In a climate where faith can be a mile long and an inch deep, this all sounds like way too much effort to be considered spiritual. But Paul (who knew something about spirituality), is on record as saying it is the grace of God that "teaches us to say 'No' to ungodliness and worldly passions, and to live self-controlled, upright and godly lives" (Titus 2:11-12 NIV). He tells Timothy that "God gave us a spirit not of fear but of power and love and self-control" (2 Timothy 1:7 NIV).

God's grace and the Spirit who is holy call us to discipled (disciplined) lives! We won't fall in love with discipline, or make it an end in itself, but we'll live lives of self-control because of our love for Christ.

QUESTIONS

1. Which of Dahl's areas (worship, work, play) is the most challenging for you to keep in balance?
2. What are some things that keep you from "going out too far?"

BETTER THAN A HALLELUJAH

"Hallelujah! For the Lord our God the Almighty reigns. Let us rejoice and exult and give him the glory" (19:6-7).

It might come as a bit of a surprise that, in a book with several praise sections, the word "Hallelujah" only appears four times—and all of those occurrences are clustered in the first six verses of Revelation 19. Hallelujah is a compound of two Hebrew words: hallel meaning "praise," and jah, a shortened form of Yahweh. Put it together, and it means "praise Yahweh."

The word is rooted in the Psalms. In fact, there is a section of Psalms (113-118) that is known as the Hallel. These psalms were frequently recited during times of joy and thanksgiving. And that brings us to John's employment of the word in Revelation 19. It is an occasion of unmitigated celebration.

John has shown the doom of Babylon (Rome) in several ways: the bowls of wrath being poured out on it (Revelation 16), internal divisions that would lead to its destruction (17:16), its graveyard status (18:2), and how those who profited from it would weep over their loss of revenue (rather than the Empire) when it is destroyed (18:9-19). Rome is going down! In 19:1-8, we return to "the great multitude" we saw in 7:1ff and 14:1ff. They are before the throne of God and praising Him. Their praise takes the form of three hallelujahs.

The first hallelujah is a recognition that "salvation and glory and power" belong to God because of the justness of His judgments as witnessed in the downfall of Rome and the avenging of the saints (vv. 1-2). God is worthy of praise because He has done praiseworthy things. And what He has specifically done is reward those who have put their hope in Him. In the judgment on Rome, He has validated everything the saints were suffering for.

The patient endurance repeatedly called for in Revelation (1:9; 3:10; 13:10; 14:12) is predicated on the hope that God "rewards those who seek him" (Hebrews 11:6 NIV). The disciples displayed this hope by practicing righteousness (19:7-8) in the face of powerful and daunting opposition. When hard times came and loss set in, they fixed their hearts on things that couldn't be touched or taken. For some of our first-century family, there was nothing left for them to hold on to other than their hope. But hold on they did, and in this judgment their hope is realized. That's worth a "Hallelujah," don't you think?

The second "Hallelujah" is about how "the smoke from her goes up forever and ever, " (v. 3). This is praise for God making His way known and manifested to all who are willing to see it. What happens to the wicked? What is the end for those who live in rebellion to God? Take a look at Rome, and you have the answer! Its end and judgment stand as an example of what happens to all of the ungodly. There is no reason for anyone to be in doubt or to wonder.

At this point, the 24 elders and the four living creatures around the throne echo this "Hallelujah" and add an "Amen" to it. As those closest to God, we're being told that the first two "Hallelujahs" of the saints are spot on. They know exactly what they're talking about.

The final "Hallelujah" is a conclusive one. "The Lord our God the Almighty reigns" (v. 6 NIV). It's not that God wasn't reigning before Rome's fall; it's just that, in this judgment, God's rule has been reaffirmed. There are two words worthy of special note here. The first is "Almighty." Rome's fall, as predicted as long ago as Daniel 2, left no doubt as to Who has the power—it is not the Eternal City, it is the eternal God. But notice it's "Our" Lord God Almighty who is reigning. It's not some impersonal force or an abstract deity, but the God who reaches out through His Son and enters into relationship with us. You want to know how our brothers and sisters made it through hard times? The answer is their Almighty Father led them.

And in the end, all of our hallelujahs and amens are sweet before His throne. But even then, they seem inadequate in light of who He is and all He has done for us. For He is, to turn the words of a popular song another way, better than a hallelujah.

QUESTIONS

1. What does the word "Hallelujah" mean? What do you tend to think of when you hear it?
2. Which of the hallelujahs in this chapter says the most to you? Why?

HERE COMES THE BRIDE!

***"For the marriage of the Lamb has come, and his Bride has made herself ready; it was granted her to clothe herself with fine linen"* (19:7-8).**

It was the moment in the wedding. The radiant bridesmaids had taken their stroll down the aisle. The adorable flower girl followed, strewing her petals of red everywhere.

Then the music stopped. The attendants stood poised, watching, anticipating the moment the double doors would open, and the bride would appear.

Finally, the music sounded, the audience rose, the doors opened, and there she was! Tears were streaming down her face, but there was no sadness here—not on this day. This was her day! All of the planning, praying, waiting, and longing were fulfilled. Hope was blooming into history in front of her eyes.

And was it worth it? Was it worth keeping herself pure? Was it worth denying herself? Was it worth waiting? Oh, how it was worth it! All of her doubts, dreams, and struggles were being answered in this single moment, and her joy was overwhelming.

That's the picture we see in Revelation 19:6-9! In the final of three hallelujahs spoken by the great multitude (vv. 1, 6), the reign of God (as manifested by the judgment on Babylon/Rome) is the occasion of gladness, rejoicing, and giving glory. The image John employs for this is of the bride meeting her groom.

If you stop and think about it, it's a great image. From John's time down to ours, weddings have been occasions of great joy and celebration. This is true for those who are invited (v. 9) as well as for those who are involved (v. 7), because they are all celebrating the same thing: the joy of the bride and groom.

Another thing John would have us to see through his use of this symbol is the realization of something that has been long anticipated and hoped for. Brides look forward to their weddings from the time they are little girls—long before they have any idea who the groom will be! When the wedding finally arrives, the joy and celebration are in proportion to their anticipation.

This picture then sums up well the joy of deliverance the saints experience in their rescue from Rome. In 6:9ff those who have been martyred ask in a "loud voice" how long it will be before judgment/vengeance comes. They are told to be patient and wait. Now we see their joy as justice is finally realized and evil dealt with in the manner which it deserves.

There's something here for the church today. Followers of Jesus experience a significant amount of persecution in certain parts of the world (North Korea, Syria, Iran, Iraq, etc.). Most people are surprised by this, since little of it is reported by the Western media. In that sense, the believers experiencing these hardships are like those of the first century—their pleas and protests are heard only by God.

But they are heard. And this text, as well as the whole of Revelation, tells them and us that evil won't prevail long. Wrongs will be righted. The faithful will be vindicated. Maybe it will happen in this life, maybe in the next—but it will happen.

Disciples are to hold on for the joy of that moment!

QUESTIONS

1. What is the wedding of the Lamb and His bride meant to symbolize? In what ways is this an effective symbol?
2. What does the “fine linen” stand for (v. 8)? How does that speak to disciples today?

THE REIGN OF HOPE

***"Blessed and holy is the one who shares in the first resurrection! Over such the second death has no power, but they will be priests of God and of Christ, and they will reign with him for a thousand years"* (20:6).**

If you've made it this far, you know that the Battle of Armageddon that began in Revelation 16 has been concluded in Revelation 19. The two beasts have been thrown into the lake of fire. All of the pictures and images associated with Rome's judgment are finished with one exception: Satan has not been dealt with. It stands to reason that the one who is ultimately behind the evil of Rome would be the last one punished.

Revelation 20 breaks down into three scenes. The first is the thousand-year binding of Satan and corresponding reign with Christ of His disciples (living and dead). A thousand years is no more an amount of time than the 3½ years we saw used earlier (see p. 124ff). It stands for fullness and totality of victory. With Rome's defeat, Satan has been conquered. His key to the Abyss (9:1) has been taken, and the place he controlled is now the place where he is controlled. On the throne are those who "had been given authority to judge" (v. 4 NIV), i.e., those who have overcome (2:26; 3:21). The disciples who died have been resurrected and share in this reign (v. 4).

The second image is Satan being released and enlisting Gog and Magog to do battle against the people of God (vv. 7-9). He is defeated and thrown into the same lake of fire as the beast and false prophet (v. 10). If the first image deals with Satan's defeat through Rome, this picture deals with his defeat after Rome and answers the question, "What happens whenever Satan manifests himself in the future?" The answer is: the same thing that happened with Rome. No matter how or when he appears, he will be defeated.

The last picture is of judgment. But in the context, it is not what happens at the end of time, but is entirely Rome-related and comes from Daniel 7:9-11. We were told earlier that those saints who were part of the first resurrection could not be touched by the second death (v. 6). Since they were part of a first resurrection, the group now spoken of is part of the second resurrection (see them alluded to in v. 5). Who are they? They are those who fought on the side of the beast (19:19). They were killed (v. 21) and now they are resurrected to experience a second death in the lake of fire. They're not righteous, so their resurrection is separated and distinguished from the earlier resurrection of those who died in faithfulness to Jesus. With their judgment, every remnant of Rome is gone. This is why we're told, "From his presence earth and sky fled away, and no place was found for them" (20:11 NIV). The world of Rome is no more.

In three scenes, we've seen the end of Satan as well as those who fought against Jesus. We've also seen the ultimate triumph of those on the side of the Lamb. The trust they displayed in their Lord was not in vain. The reign of Christ is a reign of hope.

QUESTIONS

1. Should we understand the thousand years as literal? Why or why not? What does it represent?
2. Is the judgment scene at the end of Revelation 20 the final judgment? Why or why not?
3. What hope would this chapter provide for the first-century disciples who received this letter? What hope does it give us?

FAQ

How is Satan's future work after Rome—i.e., his being set free in v. 3 to "deceive the nations" (v. 8)—said to be for "a short time."

Remember, we're in the middle of a series of pictures. The "short time" is not to be literalized and understood as the time between the fall of Rome and the final return of Jesus. In the picture before us, it is simply enough time/opportunity to raise another army (Gog and Magog) to go against the people of God (v. 9).

Who are Gog and Magog?

This comes to us from Ezekiel 38-39. There, the Jews have been taken away into exile, but God promises a future return and restoration of their kingdom under David (a figure for Jesus). To assure them this will happen, he poses a worst-case scenario: Gog from Magog moves in to wage war against them.

Gog from Magog answers to no historical reality. He is the leader of an idealized army of "horsemen fully armed" (38:4 NIV), a great horde with swords and shields, and allies from many nations. They are like a cloud covering the land (v. 9). Despite all of this, they are defeated, not by Judah, but by God (vv. 18-23).

The point of this is to assure Israel that no one can stop God from accomplishing His plans (39:25-29). God is telling them to think of the worst enemy they can and know that He will defeat them, for He is able to do beyond what they can think or imagine (Ephesians 3:20-21). This is also the way Gog and Magog are used in Revelation 20 (McGuiggan). Satan has been defeated in Rome, but what if he somehow comes again against God's people? This is why he "deceives" Gog and Magog to go against the people of God, and why they are defeated; to show that no matter what comes up against the people of God, they will triumph through Jesus.

Are you sure 20:11-15 isn't referring to the final judgment?

There are a couple of significant issues that arise if we interpret these verses to be the final judgment. First of all, the only people who are resurrected and judged are the wicked; the righteous were raised in the first resurrection (vv. 4-6). In light of John 5:28-29, this alone should be enough to cause us to question such a reading.

Another issue mentioned earlier is that this picture comes to us from Daniel 7:9-11 where it clearly deals with the defeat of the fourth kingdom (v. 23-27), not the final judgment. It wouldn't be impossible for John to use the picture in a different way than Daniel does, but we've already seen in Revelation 17 that's not how he treats Daniel 7. He understands it as the prequel to his vision. There's no good reason to deviate from that here.

Saints being resurrected to reign for a thousand years, Satan being released from prison, Gog and Magog—we're clearly in a section of pictures in a book of images. There's no reason to start literalizing here.

What have we seen?

We've seen the bowls of wrath poured out and looked at Rome's demise from several vantage points. We've heard Rome lamented over by those who stood to profit from their relationship, while the great multitude of Jesus' followers raised a chorus of hallelujahs. Finally, we've seen Satan dealt with in such a way that the church, then and now, is assured that he will never be victorious.

Hallelujah!

PART SEVEN

The God Who Makes All Things New

We've reached the end of the journey, and what a journey it's been! What John sees next, if isolated from its context, could be taken as a description of heaven—but it's not. When you look carefully at what is being said, it's evident that he is describing the freedom and liberation brought to the people of God. They have experienced deliverance from Rome, so the language employed to describe it intersects with what we might expect to hear in regard to our ultimate deliverance in heaven.

The triumphant church in four pictures (21:1-22:5)
Final words from an angel, John, and Jesus (22:6-21)

A GLORIOUS CITY, A BEAUTIFUL BRIDE, & EDEN

"Then I saw a new heaven and a new earth, for the first heaven and the first earth had passed away, and the sea was no more. And I saw the holy city, new Jerusalem, coming down out of heaven from God, prepared as a bride adorned for her husband" **(21:1-2).**

Revelation 21-22 paints a picture of the people of God (the church) in glorious deliverance and triumph. It is not heaven. In the scene of judgment upon Rome in 20:11-12, we were told, "From his presence earth and sky fled away, and no place was found for them." "Heaven and earth" is compressed biblical speech for someone's world. When a nation opposes God, their "world" is inevitably destroyed (cf. Babylon, Isaiah 13:1ff; Edom, Isaiah 34:1ff; Nineveh, Nahum 1:1ff; Judah, Zephaniah 1:1ff). In this case, it is the Roman world that flees from God's presence.

I think McGuiggan (upon whom I've leaned heavily here), has it right when he points out that if "world" destruction is a sign of curse, then the creation of a "new world" is the language of blessing. In biblical parlance, it's a new heaven and earth. It is not a literal new world any more than the person who comes to Christ becomes a literal new person (2 Corinthians 5:17), but the old world experiencing a new set of circumstances and manner of existence. In 21:1ff, it is freedom from oppression under Domitian. Notice how it's specifically pointed out that "there was no longer any sea" (v. 1 NIV). According to 13:1, the sea is where the beast came from (McGuiggan). In this new world, there is none of that; the previous heaven and earth have passed away (22:1). There will be no more death, mourning, crying, or pain from Rome, for "the old order of things has passed away" (v. 4 NIV). John is picturing the deliverance the church enjoys, not in eternity, but in history (remember he's speaking to seven churches in first-century Asia).

Having said that, it's not clear to me whether the dominant image for the delivered church is that of the glorious city or the beautiful bride. Maybe the answer is both, for he sees "the holy city, new Jerusalem, coming down out of heaven from God, prepared as a bride adorned for her husband" (21:2 NIV). The city is the bride, and the bride is the city (vv. 9-10), and the images shift according to the particular truth being emphasized. Does he wish to stress how the people of God "look" to God and the intimacy they enjoy with the Father? They are a bride "adorned for her husband" and God dwells with them and makes His vows (vv. 3-4). Does John want to say something about their security and preciousness? They are a city with walls 1,400 miles high and 200 feet thick, with foundations decorated with every kind of precious stone (vv. 16-17, 19). These pictures said marvelous things to the churches of Asia and to churches today!

In 22:1-5, the city image is further developed as we're told of a river and a tree within it. This is Eden, and it illustrates what was said in 21:5 when "He who was seated on the throne said, 'Behold, I am making all things new'" (NIV) The tree bears fruit each month for those within the city, but its leaves are for the healing of the nations. If this were heaven, there would be no need for healing, but because it's the church, this is essentially Revelation's version of the Great Commission. The tree of life that nourishes the saints is not just for them—it is also for the world! The jewels adorning the walls of the city are the same as those on the high priest's breastplate (Exodus 28:17-20). Just as those stones were to remind him of the people he was representing before God, the twelve stones in the city remind the church of their mission to the world (Aune). The church has previously been told that "the nations will walk by its light" (i.e., the light of the city, 21:23-24 NIV). The Spirit and the bride say, "Come" (22:17). Even in this idyllic picture, the people of God are reminded they do not exist for themselves!

Revelation is not escapist literature!

QUESTIONS

1. What is the new heaven and new earth? How is this the language of blessing?
2. What do the symbols of the church as a bride and a city speak to? What do they tell us about how God looks at the church?
3. What elements of outreach do we see in this picture?

FAQ

If there was further Roman persecution on the horizon, how can John speak of the disciples being delivered into a new heaven and a new earth (i.e., being free from Rome)?

In the same way that Satan (who has been defeated by Christ, yet still wars against us) can be spoken of as a defeated foe (because he is!). On the basis of Jesus' obedience to God, we have been delivered by Christ into a new existence (John 3:3ff; 2 Corinthians 5:17). We still have to resist Satan, but a substantial part of the way we do so is by realizing that he is a defeated foe (1 John 2:13-14; 3:8). Things are not the same after the cross as they were before!

With the death of Domitian, Jesus comes in judgment upon Rome and delivers His followers into a new world. The Senate (rather than declare his deity, as with previous emperors) instead issues a *damnatio memoriae* and all traces of him are removed from the Temple of the Sebastoi in Ephesus as well as from statues, temples, altars, arches, and public records throughout the Empire. Nerva, Domitian's successor, limits the *Fiscus Judaicus* to practicing Jews and issues a coin proclaiming, "Abolition of malicious prosecution in connection with the Jewish tax," so that non-Jewish people cannot be prosecuted as "atheists" (Heemstra). Rome will still be around for a while, but things are not the same as they were! The saints have been delivered!

GETTING OUT OF THE WAY

"No longer will there be anything accursed, but the throne of God and of the Lamb will be in it, and his servants will worship him. They will see his face, and his name will be on their foreheads. And night will be no more. They will need no light of lamp or sun, for the Lord God will be their light, and they will reign forever and ever" (22:3-5).

Revelation 21-22 are rich in truths that speak to our circumstances right now. While I don't have an issue with anyone who wants to find in these chapters some principles that also apply to heaven, I am afraid that because this material is usually understood as speaking exclusively of our future existence, it too often serves no purpose other than to "describe" heaven to us. Maybe that's overstating things; I suppose it can also awaken or re-energize our desire and hope for being with God, and that's certainly not a bad thing.

Still, if we use these chapters only to celebrate a future existence, I think we have missed much of the importance of the text. Maybe the place to begin is by returning to the messages Jesus gives the seven churches and recognizing that the promises He makes to those who overcome are fulfilled not in heaven, but in the church. While not every single item is explicitly mentioned, it's nonetheless clear that we're to see what is promised to those who overcome in Revelation 2-3 is fulfilled in their deliverance from Rome. Here's a chart that pulls this together.

Promise	**Fulfillment**
Eat from the tree of life in paradise (2:7)	22:1-2, 14
Not be hurt by the second death (2:11)	21:7-8
Hidden manna, white stone, new name (2:17)	22:4
Authority over the nations, the morning star (2:26-27)	21:24-22:5, 16
Dressed in white, name in book of life (3:5)	22:14, 19; 21:27
Make pillar in the temple of God, write on them My name (3:12)	22:4
The right to sit with Jesus on His throne (3:21)	22:5

What this suggests is that many have underestimated their status on earth as followers of the Lamb! Appearances would suggest that we're extraordinarily ordinary: three songs and a prayer. The reality John would have us see is much different. When we were united with the Lord at baptism, "God raised us up with Christ and seated us with him in the heavenly realms in Christ Jesus" (Ephesians 2:6 NIV). This is where our citizenship is, not just will be (Philippians 3:20-21). We've already noted how followers of Jesus are not just said to dwell in heaven (12:12; 13:6); they are pictured as being there!

Russell Conwell tells the story of Ali Hafed in his book, *Acres of Diamonds*. Hafed was a content, wealthy man until he developed an insatiable appetite for diamonds. His obsession led him to sell his farm and all that he owned and spend his entire fortune traveling the world in search of diamonds. He died a penniless, broken man in a foreign land. What happened to the man who purchased Hafed's farm? He found that the land contained ... acres of diamonds. Hafed was in possession of great riches all along; he just failed to realize it.

I have no wish to minimize the glories of our future life. Who would? They will be out of this world in more than one sense. But I do think we can fail to see and appreciate the present glories of the kingdom. These realities are embraced by faith, not by sight. They flow out of our relationship with God and others and transcend the crying babies in the assembly, small crowds on Sunday night, and the off-key singing of the person behind you. And though some don't act like it, the kingdom of heaven doesn't need a mega-church, mega-preacher, mega-facilities, or mega-programs to embellish its glory. When you have a Lord and Savior like ours, the best thing we can do is get out of the way.

QUESTIONS

1. Can you think of a time when you've ever heard Revelation 22 used in a message or Bible class? Do you remember in what context it was used?
2. What things get in the way of us seeing the glory of God's kingdom? How can we work past such things?

3 WITNESSES, 2 WORDS, & 1 READER

"And he said to me, 'Do not seal up the words of the prophecy of this book, for the time is near'" (22:10).

As John concludes Revelation, we hear three witnesses testify to the truth of his vision. The first is an angel, one of the seven who poured out the bowls of wrath (21:9). We are assured by him that the words of the book are "trustworthy and true," and that he was sent to show the servants of God the things that will soon occur (v. 6).

John speaks next. He is so awestruck by all that he has seen and heard that he falls at the feet of the angel to worship until he is reminded that only God is worthy of such—something we'd do well to remember in our celebrity culture where sports figures, movie stars, musicians, and others are often held up in a way that isn't good for them or us. John repeats what the angel has said about not sealing up the words of the prophecy because the time is near.

Finally, Jesus speaks. He also reminds us of the nearness of His coming and of His ability to get the job done. He pronounces a blessing on those who "wash their robes" (v. 14). He then affirms that He has sent His angel to give this testimony for the churches.

I'm sure one of the things we're to get from all of this is the reality and reliability of this prophetic word. By the mouth of three witnesses, everything has been confirmed (Deuteronomy 19:15). Difficult days were coming, and when they did, the churches would need to know that John's message was a sure guide for uncertain times.

Closely connected to this is the immediacy with which all of these things were going to happen. It's not just that they needed this prophetic message somewhere down the road; things were going to start happening soon, so they needed it now. This speaks to urgency.

Revelation closes, then, with three witnesses reminding seven churches that God's word through John was real and relevant. I can't help but think that this is at least part of the message we need to embrace in regard to Revelation. Too often, it sits in the back of our Bibles, and we pass through it only on our way to maps. That's no good. In the words of the angel, we have sealed up the book.

It's also worth noting that this message is placed at the end of the book in addition to the beginning. At the beginning, we need encouragement to continue through the book. At the end, we need encouragement to understand how what was said is vital to our lives. So as we near the book's conclusion, I challenge you who have made it through Revelation to do something about it. Be strengthened by the hope it offers. Share it. Teach it. Let people know the wealth of blessing that awaits the one who is willing to give it a patient hearing.

QUESTIONS

1. Who are the three witnesses in this section? What is their message?
2. What are some of the blessings you've received from studying Revelation? What do you plan to do with what you've learned?

"COME!"

"The Spirit and the Bride say, 'Come.' And let the one who hears say, 'Come.' And let the one who is thirsty come; let the one who desires take the water of life without price" **(22:17).**

In a book that's chock-full of dragons, plagues, angels, beasts coming out of the sea and earth, and much more, it's easy to overlook some of the quieter passages in Revelation. But we do so to our impoverishment. The above passage may speak softly in comparison to the imagery and action of other texts, but it is rich in its message to us.

This invitation occurs in the context of Jesus promising to come in judgment and "repay each one for what he has done" (v. 12 NIV). While this is meant to bring terror to the hearts of the impenitent, it would be welcome news to the bone-weary disciple suffering because of their faithfulness; their fidelity was about to be rewarded! Then Jesus adds, "Blessed are those who wash their robes, so that they may have the right to the tree of life and that they may enter the city by the gates" (v. 14). This serves as a preamble to the invitation.

The invitation is given by the Spirit and the bride. Together they say, "Come." There are (at least) two big truths here. One is that, whenever the church extends the good news to someone, it is in partnership with the Spirit. There are no solos, just duets. Notice, too, the simplicity of the invitation: "Come." It is not a summons to do the impossible or to do nothing at all. It is to do what we are all capable of doing—walk with Jesus. For most, this will not be easy, for implicit in the call is a directive to leave behind whatever might prevent us from following (Luke 14:25ff).

"The one who hears" is the member of one of the seven churches hearing John's words read. They are already following, and because they are, they will be inviters. They join with the Spirit and the rest of the church. Everyone in the kingdom is united in inviting the world to come.

Who should come? The one who wishes to drink the free water of life. For the people of this time and place, the scarcity of water made this an incredibly rich figure. But it's not just any water that's being offered; this is water that satisfies the thirst for life, so the image speaks to all who long for something more than just existence and seek a purpose greater than themselves. It's the kind of thing Mark Twain was speaking of when he said, "The two most important days in your life are the day you were born and the day you find out why. " That day arrives when people "come" in response to the Spirit's invitation.

Through Jesus Christ, the Almighty of the universe invites us to Himself.

"Come."

QUESTIONS

1. "How is the word "come" a fitting invitation to discipleship? In what ways have you come to Jesus? In what ways can we invite others to "come" to the Lord?
2. Have you ever thought of being partners with the Spirit when you share the good news with someone? How does knowing this help you?

What have we seen?

Really—what haven't we seen? What an ending! What a book!

We've seen seven churches of Asia standing toe-to-toe with the mighty Roman Empire as driven by the forces of Satan. When the smoke and ashes had cleared, the seven churches remained, and Rome had gone down to defeat. Rome's lord was no match for the church's Lord!

We've seen the triumphant church pictured as a new heaven and earth, a glorious city, a beautiful bride, and Eden. We've heard the angel, the apostle, and Jesus testify to the truthfulness of all that is in the book. We've seen victory as great as any we'll ever see...

Until we see Him!

AFTERWORD

A few years ago I came across a video on YouTube of a man playing a piano while a woman sings "O Holy Night."[1] Part of what makes this clip special has to do with the person playing the piano—Billy Preston. Preston was a wonder on the keyboards. There wasn't anything he couldn't do. He had a career as a solo artist, but he was best known for recording, playing, or touring with all of the big names: Sam Cooke, Aretha Franklin, Ray Charles, Mahalia Jackson, Little Richard, The Beatles, Bob Dylan, The Rolling Stones, and Eric Clapton. He also wrote the song, "You Are So Beautiful." This guy had big-time talent.

But if Preston was remarkably gifted, he also had his share of pain and problems in life. Much of it was self-inflicted (drugs, insurance fraud, and other run-ins with the law). He had a self-destructive side that seemed to get the better of him as the years went on. He died in 2006 at the age of 59, his body worn out from a lifetime of abuse.

I suppose his close friends knew this and did what they could to help and encourage him. That's where this video comes in. Preston and Franklin had known each other since their teenage years, and it shows in how comfortable they are around each other. There's no friend like an old friend, is there?

---

1. At the time of this writing, this was available on YouTube. The video quality is not the best, but Aretha and Billy are special to watch under any condition.

What I especially like about this clip is the joy I see in Billy Preston. During the final minute or so of the song, it's obvious that he is caught up in the moment, the music, and Aretha's powerful rendition of the song. He's bobbing his head, looking at her, and smiling. I like the way Aretha keeps her arm around Preston's shoulder for nearly the entire song. There's nothing phony or staged about it; it is the sincere gesture of a friend, someone who maybe thinks of herself as an older sister to Preston. Anyway, it's poignant. It's almost as if Aretha (no stranger to hard times herself) can sense the pain that's part of Preston's life and wants to comfort him and try to keep him from it. Thank God for sisters like that.

And oh yeah, the song isn't too bad either. Aretha can sing, Billy can play, and they do it quite well together. I especially like the part that says:

Long lay the world in sin and error pining,
Till He appeared and the soul felt its worth.

The truth is, we were all Billy Prestons in this world, locked into our own sinful, self-destructive, and others-destructive ways. Christ appeared and told us, "You don't have to live this way. I made you to be something better!" And then He showed us what we were made for by the kind of life He lived. We had no idea we had been created for such a high and lofty purpose, and when we learned this, we felt our worth and fell on our knees.

I know you can analyze things like this too much, or you can take it in a different direction than the circumstances warrant. Qualify this any way you need to, but don't miss the central thrust: all the tenderness and trueness of love that you see in this video and hear in this song is in Jesus Christ. It is at the cross that He puts His arms around us, looks unflinchingly into our eyes, and calls us to something better. There's no soft bigotry of low expectations with Him (Gerson) —He knows we're made for more!

The thrill of hope—a weary world rejoices,
For yonder breaks a new and glorious morn.
Fall on your knees! Oh hear the angel voices!
Oh night divine! Oh night when Christ was born!

When you know you're made for something more, and that something is life with God, you're ready for the birth of water and the Spirit into the kingdom of God (John 3:3ff). The book of Acts is filled with examples of men and women submitting to this new birth (2:37ff; 8:12-13; 16:13-15). If you haven't taken this step, I urge you to do so and to know that joy that comes from belonging to Him (Acts 8:26-39; 16:29-34).

SELECTED BIBLIOGRAPHY

Aune, David E., *Revelation,* 3 Volumes (Word Biblical Commentary series). Thomas Nelson, 1997-98.

Barclay, William, *The Revelation of John,* 2 Volumes. The Westminster Press, 1960, 1976.

Bauckham, Richard, *The Theology of the Book of Revelation.* Cambridge University Press, 1998.

Carter, Warren, *The Roman Empire and the New Testament.* Abingdom Press, 2006.

Eusebius, *The History of the Church.* Dorset Press, 1984.

Ferguson, Everett, *Backgrounds of Early Christianity* (3rd edition). Wm. B. Eerdman's Publishing Co., 2003.

Friesen, Steven J., *Imperial Cults and the Apocalypse of John.* Oxford University Press, 2001.

Gifford, Dave, *Giffmex's Blog of Apoca-Lists,* http://www.revelation.giffmex.org, 2010.

Gorman, Michael J., *Reading Revelation Responsibly.* Cascade Books, 2011.

Hailey, Homer, *Revelation.* Baker Book House, 1979.

Harland, Philip A., *Associations, Synagogues, and Congregations.* Online Edition, 2013.

Heemstra, Marius, The Interpretation and Wider Context of Nerva's Fiscus Judaicus Sesterius, www.academia.edu, 2010.

Hemer, Colin J., *The Letters to the Seven Churches of Asia in Their Local Setting.* Wm. B. Eerdman's Publishing Co., 2001.

Jones, Brian, *Emperor Domitian.* Taylor & Francis e-Library, 2002.

Kim, Seyoon, *Christ and Caesar.* Wm. B. Eerdman's Publishing Co., 2008.

McGuiggan, Jim, *The Book of Daniel,* The Montex Publishing Company, 1978.

McGuiggan, Jim, *The Book of Ezekiel,* The Montex Publishing Company, 1984.

McGuiggan, Jim, *The Book of Revelation,* The Montex Publishing Company, 1978.

McGuiggan, Jim, *Celebrating the Wrath of God,* WaterBrook Press, 2001.

Oster, Richard E., Jr., *Seven Congregations in a Roman Crucible.* Wipf & Stock, 2013.

Peterson, Eugene H., *Reversed Thunder.* HarperOne, 1988.

Ramsay, William, *The Letters to the Seven Churches.* Baker Book House, 1985.

Rogers, Richard, *Hallelujah Anyway.* Sentinel Publishing Company, 1966.

Rossing, Barbara, *The Rapture Exposed.* Basic Books, 2004.

Shelly, Rubel, *The Lamb and His Enemies,* 20th Century Christian Foundation, 1983.

Schussler Fiorenza, Elisabeth. *Justice and Judgment,* Fortress Press, 1998.

Stevenson, Gregory, *A Slaughtered Lamb.* ACU Press, 2013.

Suetonius, *The Twelve Caesars*. The Folio Society, 2005.

Swete, Henry Barclay, *Commentary on Revelation*. Kregel Publications, 1977.

Tacitus, *Annals and Histories*. Alfred A Knopf, 2009.

Wright, N.T., *Revelation for Everyone*. Westminster John Knox Press, 2011.

Made in the USA
San Bernardino, CA
04 March 2016